Collins
My First
English-English-Hindi
Dictionary
अंग्रेज़ी–अंग्रेज़ी–हिन्दी

Exclusively Distributed in the Indian subcontinent by Ratna Sagar

HarperCollins Publishers
Westerhill Road
Bishopbriggs
Glasgow
G64 2QT

First edition 2011

Reprint 10 9 8 7 6 5 4 3 2 1 0

© HarperCollins Publishers 2011

ISBN   978-0-00-741562-5

www.collinslanguage.com

A catalogue record for this book is available
from the British Library

Artwork and design by Q2A Media

Printed in India by Gopsons Papers Ltd

Images used under licence from
Shutterstock.com

Editorial consultant
Professor Udaya Narayana Singh
Pro-Vice-Chancellor and Director,
Rabindra Bhavana, Visva-Bharati University

Translation co-ordination
Ajit Shirodkar

Translators
Sumit Kumar
Amrita Rao

Editors
Shalini Bansal
Suchitra Choudhury-Talukdar
Gerry Breslin
Lucy Cooper
Kerry Ferguson
Anne Robertson

Editor-in-chief
Dr Elaine Higgleton

इस शब्दकोष में कोई शब्द कैसे ढूंढा जाए

ate

⇨ Look at **eat**.

*He **ate** three apples.*

atlas *noun*
atlases

An **atlas** is a book of maps.
मानचित्र पुस्तिका

attack *verb*
attacks, attacking, attacked

If someone **attacks** another person, they try to hurt them.
हमला करना

attention *noun*

If you pay **attention**, you watch and listen.
ध्यान

*He always pays **attention** in class.*

attract *verb*
attracts, attracting, attracted

If something **attracts** things to it, it makes them move towards it.
आकर्षित करना

*Magnets **attract** anything made of iron.*

---

*I put my glass on a red **mat**.*

match *noun*
matches

1 A **match** is a small, thin stick that makes a flame when you rub it on a rough surface.
माचिस
*She lit a **match** and held it up to the candle.*

2 A **match** is a game of football, cricket, or some other sport.
खेल प्रतियोगिता
*We won all our **matches** last year.*

match *verb*
matches, matching, matched

If one thing **matches** another, they look good together.
मेल खाना
*Do these shoes **match** my dress?*

यदि आप अक्षरों का वर्णानुक्रम जानते हैं तो शब्दकोश का इस्तेमाल करना आसान होता है।

1 पहले अक्षर पर ध्यान दें, और शब्दकोश में सही पृष्ठ ढूंढने के लिए पृष्ठ के किनारों पर देखें।

2 अब दूसरे अक्षर पर ध्यान दें, और अपनी जरूरत वाला पृष्ठ खोजने के लिए, पृष्ठ के ऊपर वाले शब्दों को देखें।

3 अपने वांछित शब्द को खोजने के लिए, अब पृष्ठ पर मौजूद शब्दों की सूची में नीचे की ओर देखते जाएं।

4 आप देख सकते हैं कि शब्दों की वर्तनी कैसे की जाए।

5 आप देख सकते हैं कि शब्दों को अलग-अलग तरीकों से इस्तेमाल करने पर ये किस प्रकार बदल जाते हैं।

6 आप देख सकते हैं कि शब्द का अर्थ क्या है।

7 आप हिंदी अनुवाद देख सकते हैं।

8 आप देख सकते हैं कि कोई शब्द किस तरह वाक्य में प्रयोग किया जाता है।

9 अगर किसी शब्द के एक से ज्यादा अर्थ हैं तो आप उन्हें भी देख सकते हैं।

10 हम किसी शब्द को जाँच सकते हैं कि वह संज्ञा, क्रिया, अथवा विशेषण है। कुछ शब्दों को एक से अधिक रूप में प्रयोग कर सकते हैं।

A B C D E F G H I J K L M N O

C D E F G H I J K L M

शब्द का प्रयोग किस तरह होता है

संज्ञा

संज्ञा ऐसे शब्द होते हैं जो लोगों, स्थानों या वस्तुओं के बारे में बताते हैं।

arm *noun*
bird *noun*
car *noun*

यदि आपके पास एक से ज्यादा चीजें हैं, तो आप ऐसे शब्दों का इस्तेमाल करते हैं जिनका अंत –S(एस) से होता है।

arms
birds
cars

विशेषण

विशेषण आपको बताते हैं कि वस्तुएं, लोग या स्थान क्या होते हैं।

happy *adjective*
wild *adjective*
wet *adjective*

विशेषण को अलग-अलग तरीकों से प्रयोग किया जा सकता है।

happier, happiest
wilder, wildest
wetter, wettest

क्रिया

क्रिया ऐसे शब्द होते हैं जो आपके द्वारा किए जाने वाले कामों को बताते हैं।

eat *verb*
cry *verb*
talk *verb*

क्रिया को अलग-अलग तरीकों से प्रयोग किया जा सकता है।

eats, eating, ate, eaten
cries, crying, cried
talks, talking, talked

क्रिया को उन कामों के बारे में बताने के लिए प्रयोग किया जा सकता है जो आप अभी कर रहे हैं।

*He **teaches** people how to play the piano.*
*He **is** in the school football team.*

उनका प्रयोग उन कामों के बारे में बताने के लिए किया जा सकता है जो आपने पहले किए थे।

*She **took** the plates into the kitchen.*
*She **talked** to him on the phone.*

इसका प्रयोग उन कामों के बारे में बताने के लिए भी किया जा सकता है जो आप भविष्य में करेंगे।

*Mum **will** be angry.*
*Our teacher **will** give the prizes to the winners.*
***We'll** come along later.*

वर्तनी का उस्ताद बनने के लिए जरूरी टिप्स!

जब आप शब्दकोश में अपना वांछित शब्द ढूंढ़ लें, तो "Look, Say, Cover, Write, Check" तरीके का इस्तेमाल कर इसकी वर्तनी (स्पेलिंग) याद करने की कोशिश करें:

Look शब्द को ध्यानपूर्वक देखें।
इसकी आकृति और लंबाई को देखें।
यह देखने के लिए इसके अक्षरों पर ध्यान दें कि क्या अक्षरों का कोई ऐसा एक जैसा दोहराव है जो यह याद रखने में आपकी मदद कर सकता है कि भविष्य में इसकी वर्तनी किस तरह की जाए, उदाहरण के लिए, bright, light, tight.

Say शब्द को जोर से बोलें।
इस बारे में सोचें कि बोलने पर यह शब्द कैसा सुनाई देता है! क्या आप कोई ऐसा शब्द बोल सकते हैं जो इसकी तरह सुनाई देता है? क्या आपके शब्द में इसके जैसी ध्वनि का एक जैसा दोहराव है? शब्द को बोलें और इसकी वर्तनी करने की कोशिश करें।

Cover शब्द को ढंक दें ताकि आप इसे देख न पाएं।

Write शब्दकोश में देखे बिना यह शब्द लिखें। जब आप ऐसा करें, तो सोचें कि शब्द किस तरह दिखता है! क्या यह सही दिखाई देता है? क्या यह सही आकृति में है? क्या यह सही लंबाई में है?

Check जांच करें कि आपने इसे सही ढंग से लिखा है।

Aa

abacus *noun*
abacuses

An **abacus** is a frame with beads that move along pieces of wire. It is used for counting.
ऐबेकस/गिनतारा

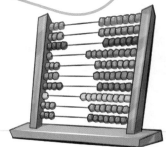

able

If you are **able** to do something, you know how to do it.
योग्य/समर्थ

*She is **able** to swim.*

about

1   **About** means to do with.
के बारे में
*This book is **about** history.*

2   **About** also means near to something.
लगभग
*His grandfather is **about** 80 years old.*

above

If something is **above** another thing, it is over it or higher than it.
ऊपर

*Lift the ball **above** your head.*

accident *noun*
accidents

1   An **accident** is something nasty that happens, and that hurts someone.
दुर्घटना
*He broke his leg in a car **accident**.*

2   If something happens by **accident**, you do not expect it to happen.
आकस्मिक/संयोग
*I dropped a cup by **accident**.*

ache *verb*
aches, aching, ached

If a part of your body **aches**, you feel a steady pain there.
दर्द

*My leg **aches** a lot.*

acorn *noun*
acorns

An **acorn** is the seed of an oak tree.
बाँजफल

across

If someone goes **across** a place, they go from one side of it to the other.
उस पार

*She walked **across** the road.*

act *verb*
acts, acting, acted

1   When you **act**, you do something.
कार्यवाही करना
*The police **acted** quickly to stop the fight.*

2   If you **act** in a play or film, you pretend to be one of the people in it.
अभिनय करना

active *adjective*

Someone who is **active** moves around a lot.
सक्रिय

*My grandmother is very **active** for her age.*

add *verb*
adds, adding, added

1   If you **add** one thing to another, you put it with the other thing.
मिलाना
***Add** the water to the flour.*

2   If you **add** numbers together, you find out how many they make together.
जोड़ना
***Add** three and six.*

address *noun*
addresses

Your **address** is the name of the place where you live.
पता

adjective *noun*
adjectives

An **adjective** is a word like "big" or "beautiful", that tells you more about a person or thing.
विशेषण

B
C
D
E
F
G
H
I
J
K
L
M
N
O
P
Q
R
S
T
U
V
W
X
Y
Z

2

admire *verb*
admires, admiring, admired

If you **admire** something, you like it and think that it is very nice or very good.
सराहना करना
*I **admired** his painting.*

adopt *verb*
adopts, adopting, adopted

If you **adopt** another person's child, you take them into your own family as your son or daughter.
गोद लेना

adult *noun*
adults

An **adult** is a person who is not a child anymore.
वयस्क

adventure *noun*
adventures

An **adventure** is something exciting which you do, or which happens to you.
रोमांचक कार्य
*He wrote a book about his **adventures** in the jungle.*

adverb *noun*
adverbs

An **adverb** is a word like "slowly", "now", or "very" that tells you about how something is done.
क्रिया-विशेषण

aeroplane *noun*
aeroplanes

An **aeroplane** is a large vehicle with wings and engines that flies through the air.
हवाई जहाज

afraid *adjective*

If you are **afraid**, you are frightened because you think that something bad will happen to you.
भयभीत
*I am not **afraid** of the dark.*

after

1 If something happens **after** another thing, it happens later than it.
बाद में
*I watched television **after** dinner.*

2 If you go **after** a person or thing, you follow them or chase them.
के पीछे
*They ran **after** her.*

afternoon *noun*
afternoons

The **afternoon** is the part of each day between twelve noon and about six o'clock.
दोपहर

again

If something happens **again**, it happens another time.
पुनः
*We went to the park **again** yesterday.*

against

1 If something is **against** another thing, it is touching it.
के सहारे
*He leaned **against** the wall.*

2 If you play **against** someone in a game, you try to beat them.
विरुद्ध
*The two teams played **against** one another.*

age *noun*
ages

Your **age** is the number of years that you have lived.
उम्र

ago

You use **ago** to talk about a time in the past.
पहले
*She left two weeks **ago**.*

agree verb
agrees, agreeing, agreed

If you **agree** with someone, you think the same as they do about something.
सहमत होना
I agree with you about him.

ahead

Someone who is **ahead** of another person is in front of them.
सामने
My brother ran ahead of us.

air noun

Air is the mixture of gases all around us that we breathe.
हवा
I opened the window and let in some air.

aircraft noun
aircraft

An **aircraft** is any vehicle which can fly.
वायुयान

airport noun
airports

An **airport** is a place where aeroplanes fly from and land.
हवाई अड्डा

alarm noun
alarms

An **alarm** is a piece of equipment that warns you of danger by making a noise.
अलार्म/चेतावनी की घंटी
The car alarm woke us up.

alien noun
aliens

In stories and films, an **alien** is a creature from another planet.
अपरदेशीय/दूसरे ग्रह का

alike adjective

If people or things are **alike**, they are the same in some way.
एक समान/सदृश
The two cats looked alike.

alive adjective

If a person, an animal or a plant is **alive**, they are living and not dead.
जीवित

all

You use **all** to talk about everything, everyone, or the whole of something.
सब
Did you eat all of it?

alligator noun
alligators

An **alligator** is a large reptile with a long body, a long mouth and sharp teeth. **Alligators'** mouths are in the shape of a letter U.
घड़ियाल

allow verb
allows, allowing, allowed

If you **allow** someone to do something, you let them do it.
अनुमति देना
Mum allowed us to go out and play.

a
b
c
d
e
f
g
h
i
j
k
l
m
n
o
p
q
r
s
t
u
v
w
x
y
z

3

A
B
C
D
E
F
G
H
I
J
K
L
M
N
O
P
Q
R
S
T
U
V
W
X
Y
Z

all right or alright *adjective*

If you say that something is **all right**, you mean that it is good enough.
ठीक-ठाक/संतोषजनक
*I thought the film was **all right**.*

almost

Almost means very nearly.
लगभग
*I **almost** missed the bus.*

alone *adjective*

When you are **alone**, you are not with any other people.
अकेला
*She was **alone** in the room.*

along

1 If you walk **along** a road or other place, you move towards one end of it.
के किनारे/समानांतर
*We walked **along** the street.*

2 If you bring something **along** when you go somewhere, you bring it with you.
साथ में
*She brought a present **along** to the party.*

aloud

When you read or talk **aloud**, you read or talk so that other people can hear you.
ऊंची आवाज़ में
*She read the story **aloud** to us.*

alphabet *noun*
alphabets

An **alphabet** is a set of letters that is used for writing words. The letters are arranged in a special order.
वर्णाक्षर
*A is the first letter of the **alphabet**.*

already

You use **already** to show that something has happened before the present time.
पहले से ही
*She is **already** here.*

also

You use **also** to give more information about something.
भी
*I'm cold, and I'm **also** hungry.*

always

If you **always** do something, you do it every time or all the time.
हमेशा
*She's **always** late for school.*

am

⇨ Look at **be**.
*I **am** six years old.*

amazing *adjective*

You say that something is **amazing** when it is a surprise and you like it.
आश्चर्यजनक
*We had an **amazing** holiday.*

ambulance *noun*
ambulances

An **ambulance** is a vehicle for taking people to hospital.
रुग्णवाहिका

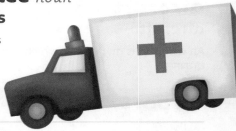

amount *noun*
amounts

An **amount** of something is how much there is of it.
राशि/मात्रा
*We only have a small **amount** of food.*

amphibian *noun*
amphibians

An **amphibian** is an animal that lives both on land and in water, for example a frog or a toad.
उभयचर

frog

4

ancient *adjective*

Ancient means very old, or from a long time ago.
प्राचीन
*They lived in an **ancient** castle.*

angry *adjective*
angrier, angriest

When you are **angry**, you feel very upset about something.
क्रोधित
*She was **angry** at her brother for breaking the window.*

animal *noun*
animals

An **animal** is any creature that is alive, but not a plant or a person.
पशु

ankle *noun*
ankles

Your **ankle** is the part of your body where your foot joins your leg.
टखना
*I fell and twisted my **ankle**.*

annoy *verb*
annoys, annoying, annoyed

If something **annoys** you, it makes you angry and upset.
खीझ दिलाना
*It **annoys** me when people are rude.*

another

You use **another** to mean one more.
एक और
*She ate **another** cake.*

answer *verb*
answers, answering, answered

If you **answer** someone, you say something back to them.
जवाब देना
*She said hello, but he didn't **answer**.*

ant *noun*
ants

Ants are small insects that live in large groups.
चींटी

antelope *noun*
antelopes

An **antelope** is an animal that looks like a deer.
चिंकारा

any

1 You use **any** to mean some of a thing.
किंचित/कुछ भी
*Is there **any** juice left?*

2 You also use **any** to show that it does not matter which one.
कोई भी
*Take **any** book you want.*

anybody

You use **anybody** to talk about a person, when it does not matter which one.
कोई/कोई व्यक्ति
*Is there **anybody** there?*

anyone

You use **anyone** to talk about a person, when it does not matter who.
कोई भी/किसी को
*Don't tell **anyone**.*

anything

You use **anything** to talk about a thing, when it does not matter which one.
कुछ भी
*I can't see **anything**.*

a b c d e f g h i j k l m n o p q r s t u v w x y z

A
B
C
D
E
F
G
H
I
J
K
L
M
N
O
P
Q
R
S
T
U
V
W
X
Y
Z

anywhere

You use **anywhere** to talk about a place, when it does not matter which one.
कहीं भी
*You can go **anywhere** you like.*

apart

1 When things are **apart**, there is a space or a distance between them.
अलग
*The desks are too far **apart**.*

2 If you take something **apart**, you take it to pieces.
अलग-अलग करना
*He took his bike **apart**.*

ape *noun*
apes

An **ape** is an animal like a large monkey with long, strong arms and no tail.
बंदर जैसा पुच्छहीन बड़ा प्राणी

apologize
or **apologise** *verb*
apologizes, apologizing, apologized

When you **apologize**, you say that you are sorry for something you have said or done.
क्षमा मांगना
*He **apologized** for breaking the window.*

appear *verb*
appears, appearing, appeared

When something **appears**, it becomes possible to see it.
दिखलाई पड़ना/प्रकट होना
*The sun **appeared** from behind the clouds.*

apple *noun*
apples

An **apple** is a firm, round fruit with green, red, or yellow skin.
सेब

April *noun*

April is the month after March and before May. It has 30 days.
अप्रैल
*His birthday is in **April**.*

apron *noun*
aprons

An **apron** is a large piece of cloth that you wear over your other clothes to keep them clean when you are cooking or painting.
पेशबंद/ऊपरी लबादा

are

➡ Look at **be**.
*They **are** both in my class.*

area *noun*
areas

An **area** is a part of a place.
क्षेत्र
*We live in an **area** near the park.*

aren't

Aren't is short for **are not**.
*My friends **aren't** here today.*

argue *verb*
argues, arguing, argued

If you **argue** with someone, you talk about something that you do not agree about.
तर्क करना/विवाद करना
*We **argued** about where to go.*

argument *noun*
arguments

If you have an **argument** with someone, you talk about something that you do not agree about.
तर्क/विवाद
*She had an **argument** with another girl.*

arm *noun*
arms

Your **arms** are the two parts of your body between your shoulders and your hands.
बाँह
*She stretched her **arms** out.*

arm

armchair *noun*
armchairs

An **armchair** is a big comfortable chair with parts on the sides for you to put your arms on.
हत्थेवाली कुर्सी

army *noun*
armies

An **army** is a large group of soldiers who fight in a war.
सेना

around

1 **Around** means in a circle.
चारों ओर
*There were lots of people **around** her.*

2 You also use **around** to say that something is in every part of a place.
चारों तरफ़/हर ओर
*His toys lay **around** the room.*

3 **Around** also means near to something.
आस-पास/लगभग
*We left **around** noon.*

arrange *verb*
arranges, arranging, arranged

1 If you **arrange** something, you make plans for it to happen.
प्रबंध करना
*We **arranged** a party for her birthday.*

2 If you **arrange** things somewhere, you put them in a way that looks tidy or pretty.
व्यवस्थित करना
*He **arranged** the books in piles.*

arrive *verb*
arrives, arriving, arrived

When you **arrive** at a place, you get there.
पहुँचना
*We **arrived** ten minutes late.*

arrow *noun*
arrows

1 An **arrow** is a long, thin stick with a sharp point at one end.
बाण/तीर
*The soldiers used bows and **arrows**.*

2 An **arrow** is also a sign that shows you which way to go.
तीर का चिह्न
*Follow the **arrows** along the path.*

art *noun*

Art is something that someone has made for people to look at, for example a painting or drawing.
कला

ask *verb*
asks, asking, asked

1 If you **ask** someone a question, you say that you want to know something.
पूछना
*I **asked** him what his name was.*

2 If you **ask** for something, you say that you want it.
माँगना
*She **asked** for some sweets.*

asleep *adjective*

If you are **asleep**, you are sleeping.
निद्रामग्न/निद्रा में
*The cat was **asleep** under the tree.*

assembly *noun*
assemblies

An **assembly** is a group of people who meet together.
सभा
*We were late for school **assembly**.*

assistant *noun*
assistants

An **assistant** is someone who helps another person in their work.
सहायक

astronaut *noun*
astronauts

An **astronaut** is a person who travels in space.
अंतरिक्षयात्री

a
b
c
d
e
f
g
h
i
j
k
l
m
n
o
p
q
r
s
t
u
v
w
x
y
z

7

A
B
C
D
E
F
G
H
I
J
K
L
M
N
O
P
Q
R
S
T
U
V
W
X
Y
Z

ate

⇨ Look at **eat**.
He ate three apples.

atlas *noun*
atlases

An **atlas** is a book of maps.
मानचित्र पुस्तिका

attack *verb*
attacks, attacking, attacked

If someone **attacks** another person, they try to hurt them.
हमला करना

attention *noun*

If you pay **attention**, you watch and listen.
ध्यान
He always pays attention in class.

attract *verb*
attracts, attracting, attracted

If something **attracts** things to it, it makes them move towards it.
आकर्षित करना
Magnets attract anything made of iron.

audience *noun*
audiences

An **audience** is all of the people who watch or listen to something, for example a film or a play.
श्रोता/दर्शक

August *noun*

August is the month after July and before September. It has 31 days.
अगस्त
We went on holiday in August.

aunt *noun*
aunts

Your **aunt** is the sister of your mother or father, or the wife of your uncle.
चाची/ताई/बुआ/मौसी/मामी

author *noun*
authors

An **author** is a person who writes books.
लेखक

autumn *noun*
autumns

Autumn is the season after summer and before winter. In the **autumn** the weather usually becomes cooler and the leaves fall off the trees.
शरद ऋतु

awake *adjective*

Someone who is **awake** is not sleeping.
जगा हुआ
I stayed awake until midnight.

away

1 If someone moves **away** from a place, they move so that they are not there any more.
दूर
He walked away from the house.

2 If you put something **away**, you put it where it should be.
जगह पर
Put your books away before you go.

awful *adjective*

If something is **awful**, it is very bad.
खराब/भद्दा
There was an awful smell.

axe *noun*
axes

An **axe** is a tool with a handle and a big, sharp blade. It is used to chop wood.
कुल्हाड़ी

Bb

baby *noun*
babies

A **baby** is a very young child.
शिशु

back *noun*
backs

1   Your **back** is the part of your body from your neck to your bottom.
पीठ
*He was lying on his **back** in the grass.*

2   The **back** of something is the side or part of it that is farthest from the front.
पिछवाड़ा
*She was in a room at the **back** of the shop.*

backwards

1   If you move **backwards**, you move in the direction behind you.
पीछे की ओर
*She walked **backwards**.*

2   If you do something **backwards**, you do it the opposite of the usual way.
उलटी ओर से
*He had his jumper on **backwards**.*

bad *adjective*
worse, worst

1   Something that is **bad** is not nice or good.
ख़राब
*The weather is **bad** today.*

2   Someone who is **bad** does things they should not do.
बुरा
*Some **bad** boys stole the money.*

badge *noun*
badges

A **badge** is a small piece of metal or plastic with words or a picture on it that you wear on your clothes.
बिल्ला

badger *noun*
badgers

A **badger** is an animal that has a white head with two black stripes on it. **Badgers** live beneath the ground and come out at night.
बिज्जू-एक पशु

bag *noun*
bags

A **bag** is a container that you use to hold or carry things.
थैला
*He put his shoes in his **bag**.*

bake *verb*
bakes, baking, baked

When you **bake** food, you cook it in an oven.
सेंकना

baker *noun*
bakers

A **baker** is a person who makes and sells bread and cakes.
नानबाई

balance *verb*
balances, balancing, balanced

When you **balance** something, you keep it steady and do not let it fall.
संतुलन
*She **balanced** a book on her head.*

ball *noun*
balls

A **ball** is a round thing that you kick, throw or catch in games.
गेंद

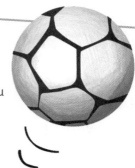

ballet *noun*

Ballet is a kind of dance with special steps that often tells a story.
बैले - एक प्रकार का नृत्य

A
B
C
D
E
F
G
H
I
J
K
L
M
N
O
P
Q
R
S
T
U
V
W
X
Y
Z

balloon *noun*
balloons

A **balloon** is a small bag made of thin rubber that you blow into to make it bigger.
गुब्बारा

banana *noun*
bananas

A **banana** is a long curved fruit with a thick yellow skin.
केला

band *noun*
bands

1 A **band** is a group of people who play music together.
संगीत मंडली
*He plays the guitar in a **band**.*

2 A **band** is also a narrow strip of material that you put around something.
फीता
*She wore a **band** round her hair.*

bandage *noun*
bandages

A **bandage** is a long strip of cloth that you wrap around a part of your body when you have hurt it.
पट्टी

bang *noun*
bangs

A **bang** is a sudden, loud noise.
धड़ाका
*The balloon burst with a **bang**.*

bank *noun*
banks

1 A **bank** is a place where people can keep their money.
बैंक
*He got some money from the **bank**.*

2 A **bank** is also the ground beside a river.
नदी का किनारा
*We walked along the **bank**.*

bar *noun*
bars

A **bar** is a long, thin piece of wood or metal.
छड़
*There were **bars** on the windows.*

bare *adjective*
barer, barest

1 If a part of your body is **bare**, it is not covered by any clothes.
नग्न
*Her feet were **bare**.*

2 If something is **bare**, it has nothing on top of it or inside it.
खाली
*The cupboard was **bare**.*

bark *verb*
barks, barking, barked

When a dog **barks**, it makes a short, loud noise.
भौंकना

barn *noun*
barns

A **barn** is a big building on a farm where animals and crops are kept.
खलिहान

base *noun*
bases

The **base** of something is the lowest part of it, or the part that it stands on.
तल
*She stood at the **base** of the stairs.*

basket *noun*
baskets

A **basket** is a container that you use to hold or carry things. It is made from thin strips of material.
टोकरी

bat *noun*
bats

1 A **bat** is a special stick that you use to hit a ball in some games.
बल्ला

2 A **bat** is also a small animal that looks like a mouse with wings. **Bats** come out to fly at night.
चमगादड़

bath *noun*
baths

A **bath** is a long container that you fill with water and sit in to wash yourself.
स्नान-कुंड

bathroom *noun*
bathrooms

A **bathroom** is a room with a bath or shower in it.
स्नान-घर

battery *noun*
batteries

A **battery** is a small tube or box for storing electricity. You put **batteries** in things like toys and radios to make them work.
बैटरी

*The clock needs a new **battery**.*

be *verb*
am, is, are, being, was, were, been

1 You use **be** to say what a person or thing is like.
   होना
   *She **is** very young.*

2 You also use **be** to say that something is there.
   होना
   *There **is** a tree in the garden.*

beach *noun*
beaches

A **beach** is the land by the edge of the sea. It is covered with sand or stones.
समुद्रतट

bead *noun*
beads

A **bead** is a small piece of glass, wood or plastic with a hole through the middle. You put **beads** on a string to make necklaces or bracelets.
मनका

beak *noun*
beaks

A bird's **beak** is the hard part of its mouth.
चोंच

bean *noun*
beans

A **bean** is the small seed of some plants that you can eat as a vegetable.
फली

bear *noun*
bears

A **bear** is a big, strong animal with thick fur and sharp claws.
भालू

beard *noun*
beards

A **beard** is the hair that grows on a man's chin and cheeks.
दाढ़ी

beat *verb*
beats, beating, beat, beaten

1 If you **beat** something, you keep hitting it.
   पीटना
   *He **beat** the drum with a stick.*

2 If you **beat** someone in a game or a competition, you do better than they do.
   हराना
   *He **beat** me in the race.*

beautiful
adjective

If something is **beautiful**, it is very nice to look at or to listen to.
सुंदर
*He painted a **beautiful** picture.*

became
⇨ Look at **become**.
*She **became** very angry.*

because

You use **because** to say why something happens.
क्योंकि
*I went to bed **because** I was tired.*

become *verb*
becomes, becoming, became, become

If one thing **becomes** another thing, it starts to be that thing.
बनना
*The weather **became** cold.*

bed *noun*
beds

A **bed** is a piece of furniture that you lie on when you sleep.
बिस्तर

bedroom *noun*
bedrooms

A **bedroom** is a room with a bed in it where you sleep.
शयनकक्ष

bedtime *noun*
bedtimes

Your **bedtime** is the time when you usually go to bed.
सोने का समय
*My **bedtime** is at eight o'clock.*

bee *noun*
bees

A **bee** is an insect with wings and black and yellow stripes on its body. **Bees** live in large groups and make honey.
मधुमक्खी

been
⇨ Look at **be**.
*We have always **been** good friends.*

beetle *noun*
beetles

A **beetle** is an insect with hard wings that cover its body when it is not flying.
गुबरैला

before

If one thing happens **before** another thing, it happens earlier than it.
पहले
*My birthday is just **before** his.*

began
⇨ Look at **begin**.
*She **began** to laugh.*

begin *verb*
begins, beginning, began, begun

If you **begin** to do something, you start to do it.
शुरू करना
*You can **begin** to write now.*

begun
⇨ Look at **begin**.
*He has **begun** to play the piano.*

behave *verb*
behaves, behaving, behaved

1   The way you **behave** is the way that you do and say things.
व्यवहार करना
*She **behaves** like a baby.*

2   If you **behave** yourself, you are good.
अच्छा आचरण करना
*You can come if you **behave** yourself.*

behind

If something is **behind** another thing, it is at the back of it.
के पीछे
*He stood **behind** his desk.*

A B C D E F G H I J K L M N O P Q R S T U V W X Y Z

believe *verb*
believes, believing, believed

If you **believe** something, you think that it is true.
विश्वास करना
*I don't **believe** that story.*

bell *noun*
bells

A **bell** is a piece of metal in the shape of a cup that rings when you shake it or hit it.
घंटी/घंटा

belong *verb*
belongs, belonging, belonged

1 If something **belongs** to you, it is yours.
संबद्ध होना
*The book **belongs** to her.*

2 If you **belong** to a group of people, you are one of them.
संबद्ध होना
*He **belongs** to our team.*

3 If something **belongs** somewhere, that is where it should be.
का होना
*Your toys **belong** in your room.*

below

If something is **below** another thing, it is lower down than it.
के नीचे
*His shoes were **below** his bed.*

belt *noun*
belts

A **belt** is a band of leather or cloth that you wear around your waist.
कमरबंद

bench *noun*
benches

A **bench** is a long seat that two or more people can sit on.
लकड़ी/पत्थर का आसन

bend *verb*
bends, bending, bent

When you **bend** something, you change its shape so that it is not straight any more.
मोड़ना
***Bend** your legs when you do this exercise.*

beneath

If something is **beneath** another thing, it is below it.
नीचे
*The dog was **beneath** the table.*

bent

⇨ Look at **bend**.
*He **bent** to pick up the bags.*

berry *noun*
berries

A **berry** is a small, soft fruit that grows on a bush or a tree.
झड़बेर

beside

If something is **beside** another thing, it is next to it.
पास में
*He sat down **beside** me.*

best

If you say that something is **best**, you mean that it is better than all the others.
सर्वश्रेष्ठ
*You are my **best** friend.*

a
b
c
d
e
f
g
h
i
j
k
l
m
n
o
p
q
r
s
t
u
v
w
x
y
z

13

better

1 You use **better** to mean that a thing is very good compared to another thing.
बेहतर
*His painting is **better** than mine.*

2 If you feel **better**, you do not feel ill any more.
बेहतर
*I feel much **better** today.*

between

If you are **between** two things, one of them is on one side of you and the other is on the other side.
के बीच में
*She stood **between** her two brothers.*

bicycle *noun*
bicycles

A **bicycle** is a vehicle with two wheels. You push the pedals with your feet to make the wheels turn.
साइकिल

big *adjective*
bigger, biggest

A person or thing that is **big** is large in size.
बड़ा
*She lives in a **big** house.*

bike *noun*
bikes

A **bike** is a bicycle or motorbike.
साइकिल/मोटरसाइकिल

bin *noun*
bins

A **bin** is a container that you put rubbish in.
कचरा-पेटी/कूड़ादान

bird *noun*
birds

A **bird** is an animal with feathers, wings, and a beak. Most **birds** can fly.
पक्षी

birthday *noun*
birthdays

Your **birthday** is the date that you were born.
जन्मदिन
*She gave me a present on my **birthday**.*

biscuit *noun*
biscuits

A **biscuit** is a kind of small, hard, dry cake.
बिस्कुट

bit *noun*
bits

A **bit** of something is a small amount of it, or a small part of it.
टुकड़ा
*I ate a **bit** of bread.*

bite *verb*
bites, biting, bit, bitten

If you **bite** something, you use your teeth to cut into it.
काटना
*The dog tried to **bite** him.*

black *noun*

Black is the colour of the sky at night.
काला
*The car is **black**.*

blackboard *noun*
blackboards

A **blackboard** is a flat, black surface that you write on with chalk in a classroom.
ब्लैकबोर्ड

blade *noun*
blades

A **blade** is the flat, sharp part of a knife that you use to cut things.
धार

blame verb
blames, blaming, blamed

If you **blame** someone for something bad, you think that they made it happen.
दोष देना
*Mum **blamed** me for making the mess.*

blanket noun
blankets

A **blanket** is a large, thick piece of cloth that you put on a bed to keep you warm.
कंबल

blew

⇨ Look at **blow**.
*The wind **blew** outside.*

blind adjective

Someone who is **blind** cannot see.
नेत्रहीन

block noun
blocks

A **block** of something is a large piece of it with straight sides.
कुंदा
*We made a house with **blocks** of wood.*

blood noun

Blood is the red liquid that moves around inside your body.
रक्त

blouse noun
blouses

A **blouse** is something a girl or woman can wear. It covers the top part of the body and has buttons down the front.
कुरती

blow verb
blows, blowing, blew, blown

1   When the wind **blows**, it moves the air.
बहना

2   When you **blow**, you push air out of your mouth.
फूँक मारना
*He **blew** on his hands to keep them warm.*

blue noun

Blue is the colour of the sky on a sunny day.
नीला
*Her dress is **blue**.*

blunt adjective
blunter, bluntest

Something that is **blunt** does not have a sharp point or edge.
धारहीन
*My pencil is **blunt**.*

boat noun
boats

A **boat** is a small vehicle that carries people on water.
नाव

body noun
bodies

A person's or animal's **body** is all their parts.
शरीर
*It's fun to stretch and twist your **body**.*

boil verb
boils, boiling, boiled

1   When water **boils**, it becomes very hot, and you can see bubbles in it and steam coming from it.
उबलना

2   When you **boil** food, you cook it in water that is boiling.
उबालना

bone noun
bones

Your **bones** are the hard parts inside your body.
हड्डी
*I broke a **bone** in my leg.*

A
B
C
D
E
F
G
H
I
J
K
L
M
N
O
P
Q
R
S
T
U
V
W
X
Y
Z

bonfire *noun*
bonfires

A **bonfire** is a big fire that is made outside.
अलाव

book *noun*
books

A **book** is a set of pages with words or pictures on them, that are held together inside a cover.
पुस्तक

boot *noun*
boots

A **boot** is a kind of shoe that covers your foot and the lower part of your leg.
ऊंचा जूता

bored *adjective*

If you are **bored**, you feel annoyed because you have nothing to do.
ऊबा हुआ

boring *adjective*

If something is **boring**, it is not interesting.
उबाऊ

born *verb*

When a baby is **born**, it comes out of its mother's body.
जन्म लेना
*My sister was **born** three years ago.*

borrow *verb*
borrows, borrowing, borrowed

If you **borrow** something from someone, they let you have it for a short time and then you give it back.
उधार लेना
*Can I **borrow** your pen, please?*

both

You use **both** to mean two people or two things together.
दोनों
*He put **both** books into the drawer.*

bottle *noun*
bottles

A **bottle** is a container made of glass or plastic that holds liquid.
बोतल

bottom *noun*
bottoms

1   The **bottom** of something is its lowest part.
    तला/पेंदी

2   Your **bottom** is the part of your body that you sit on.
    नितंब

bought

⇨ Look at **buy**.
*We **bought** bread and milk.*

bounce *verb*
bounces, bouncing, bounced

When something **bounces**, it hits another thing and then moves away from it again.
उछलना
*The ball **bounced** across the floor.*

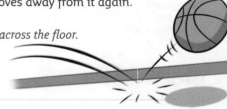

bow *verb*
bows, bowing, bowed

When you **bow**, you bend your body towards someone as a polite way of saying hello or thanking them.
झुकना
*They all **bowed** to the king.*

bow *noun*
bows

1   A **bow** is a knot with two loose ends that you use to tie laces and ribbons.
    बो/गांठ

2   A **bow** is also a long, curved piece of wood with a string stretched between the two ends, that is used to send arrows through the air.
    धनुष

bowl *noun*
bowls

A **bowl** is a round container that you use to hold food or drink.
कटोरा

box *noun*
boxes

A **box** is a container with a hard, straight bottom and sides, and usually a lid.
बक्सा

boy *noun*
boys

A **boy** is a male child.
लड़का

bracelet *noun*
bracelets

A **bracelet** is a chain or a band that you wear around your wrist.
कंगन

brain *noun*
brains

Your **brain** is inside your head. It controls your body and lets you think and feel things.
दिमाग/मस्तिष्क

branch *noun*
branches

The **branches** of a tree are the parts that grow out from its trunk and have leaves on them.
टहनी

brave *adjective*
braver, bravest

If you are **brave**, you are not afraid of something dangerous.
बहादुर/साहसी

bread *noun*

Bread is a food that is made from flour and water and baked in an oven.
पावरोटी

break *verb*
breaks, breaking, broke, broken

1 When something **breaks**, it goes into pieces.
टूटना
*I dropped a plate and it **broke**.*

2 When a machine **breaks**, it stops working.
खराब हो जाना
*My brother **broke** the television.*

breakfast *noun*
breakfasts

Breakfast is the first meal of the day.
नाश्ता

breathe *verb*
breathes, breathing, breathed

When you **breathe**, air goes in and out of your body through your nose or your mouth.
साँस लेना

brick *noun*
bricks

Bricks are small blocks of baked earth used for building.
ईंट

bride *noun*
brides

A **bride** is a woman who is getting married.
दुल्हन

bridegroom *noun*
bridegrooms

A **bridegroom** is a man who is getting married.
दूल्हा

bridge *noun*
bridges

A **bridge** is something that is built over a river, a road, or a railway so that people can get across it.
पुल

bright *adjective*
brighter, brightest

1 A **bright** colour is very easy to see.
चमकीला/भड़कीला
*She wore a **bright** red dress.*

2 Something that is **bright** shines with a lot of light.
चमकीला
*The sun is very **bright** today.*

brilliant *adjective*

Something that is **brilliant** is very good.
बहुत बढ़िया
*I thought the film was **brilliant**.*

bring *verb*
brings, bringing, brought

If you **bring** something, you take it with you when you go somewhere.
लाना
*You can **bring** a friend to the party.*

broke
⇨ Look at **break**.
*I'm sorry I **broke** the radio.*

broken *adjective*

If something is **broken**, it is in pieces.
टूटा हुआ
*All of his toys are **broken**.*

broom *noun*
brooms

A **broom** is a brush with a long handle that you use to sweep the floor.
झाड़ू

brother *noun*
brothers

Your **brother** is a boy or a man who has the same mother and father as you do.
भाई

brought
⇨ Look at **bring**.
*We **brought** some food for the picnic.*

brown *noun*

Brown is the colour of earth or wood.
भूरा
*Her eyes are dark **brown**.*

bruise *noun*
bruises

A **bruise** is a purple mark on your skin that appears if something hits a part of your body.
खरोंच/आघात
*She has a big **bruise** on her leg.*

brush *noun*
brushes

A **brush** has lots of short hairs fixed to a handle. You use a **brush** to make your hair tidy, to clean things, or to paint.
ब्रश

A
B
C
D
E
F
G
H
I
J
K
L
M
N
O
P
Q
R
S
T
U
V
W
X
Y
Z

bubble *noun*
bubbles

A **bubble** is a small ball of liquid with air inside it.
बुलबुला

bucket *noun*
buckets

A **bucket** is a deep, round container with a handle that you use to hold or carry liquids.
बाल्टी

buckle *noun*
buckles

A **buckle** is something you use to fasten a belt, a shoe or a bag.
बकसुआ

bud *noun*
buds

A **bud** is a small, new part on a tree or plant that grows into a leaf or a flower.
कली

build *verb*
builds, building, built

If you **build** something, you make it by putting the parts of it together.
निर्माण करना
*They are going to **build** the school here.*

building *noun*
buildings

A **building** is a place with walls and a roof.
भवन
*Houses, shops and schools are all **buildings**.*

built
⇨ Look at **build**.
*We **built** our house on a hill.*

bulb *noun*
bulbs

A **bulb** is the part of a lamp that is made of glass and gives out light.
बिजली का लट्टू/बल्ब

bull *noun*
bulls

A **bull** is a male cow. **Bulls** have horns.
बैल

bump *verb*
bumps, bumping, bumped

If you **bump** something, or **bump** into it, you hit it without meaning to.
टक्कर देना
*I **bumped** the table with my bag.*

bunch *noun*
bunches

A **bunch** of things is a group of them.
गुच्छा/झुंड
*He held a **bunch** of keys.*

bundle *noun*
bundles

A **bundle** is a lot of clothes, sticks or other things that are fastened together.
पुलिंदा/गठरी

buried
⇨ Look at **bury**.
*The pirates **buried** the gold beneath a tree.*

burn *verb*
burns, burning, burned, burnt

1 If you **burn** something, you destroy it or damage it with fire.
जला देना
*He **burned** all the rubbish.*

2 If you **burn** yourself, you touch something that is hot and get hurt.
जलाना/दागना
*I **burned** myself on the hot iron.*

3 If something is **burning**, it is on fire.
जलना
*The bonfire is still **burning**.*

A
B
C
D
E
F
G
H
I
J
K
L
M
N
O
P
Q
R
S
T
U
V
W
X
Y
Z

burst *verb*
bursts, bursting, burst

When something **bursts**, it breaks open suddenly.
फूटना
*The bag **burst** and everything fell out of it.*

bury *verb*
buries, burying, buried

If you **bury** something, you put it into a hole in the ground and cover it up.
गाड़ना
*Squirrels **bury** nuts to eat in the winter.*

bus *noun*
buses

A **bus** is a large vehicle that carries lots of people.
बस
*I go to school on the **bus**.*

bush *noun*
bushes

A **bush** is a plant with lots of leaves and branches that is smaller than a tree.
झाड़ी

busy *adjective*
busier, busiest

1 If you are **busy**, you have a lot of things to do.
   व्यस्त
   *We were **busy** cleaning the house.*

2 A **busy** place is full of people.
   भीड़भाड़ से भरा
   *The shops are **busy** today.*

butcher *noun*
butchers

A **butcher** is a person who sells meat.
कसाई

butter *noun*

Butter is a soft yellow and white food that is made from cream. You spread it on bread or cook with it.
मक्खन

butterfly *noun*
butterflies

A **butterfly** is an insect with four large wings.
तितली

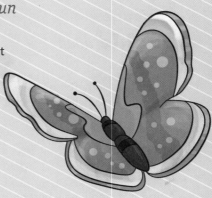

button *noun*
buttons

Buttons are small, round things on clothes that you push through holes to fasten the clothes together.
बटन

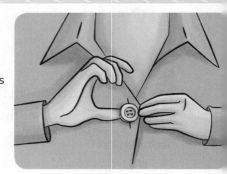

buy *verb*
buys, buying, bought

If you **buy** something, you pay money so that you can have it.
खरीदना
*We went into the shop to **buy** sweets.*

buzz *verb*
buzzes, buzzing, buzzed

If something **buzzes**, it makes a sound like a bee makes when it flies.
भिनभिनाना
*An insect **buzzed** around my head.*

20

Cc

cabbage *noun*
cabbages

A **cabbage** is a round vegetable with green, white, or purple leaves.
पत्तागोभी

cage *noun*
cages

A **cage** is a box or a room made of bars where you keep birds or animals.
पिंजड़ा

cake *noun*
cakes

A **cake** is a sweet food made from flour, eggs, sugar, and butter that you bake in an oven.
केक

calculator *noun*
calculators

A **calculator** is a small machine that you use to do sums.
परिकलक

calendar *noun*
calendars

A **calendar** is a list of all the days, weeks, and months in a year.
तिथिपत्र/कैलेंडर

calf *noun*
calves

1 A **calf** is a young cow.
बछड़ा

2 Your **calves** are also the thick parts at the backs of your legs, between your ankles and your knees.
पिंडली

call *verb*
calls, calling, called

1 If you **call** someone something, you give them a name.
पुकारना/नाम देना
I **called** *my cat Pippin.*

2 If you **call** something, you say it in a loud voice.
बुलाना
Someone **called** *his name.*

3 If you **call** someone, you talk to them on the telephone.
फ़ोन करना
I'll **call** *you tomorrow.*

calves

➪ Look at **calf**.
My **calves** *hurt.*

came

➪ Look at **come**.
My friends **came** *to play at my house.*

camel *noun*
camels

A **camel** is a large animal with one or two big lumps on its back. **Camels** live in hot, dry places and carry people and things.
ऊँट

camera *noun*
cameras

A **camera** is a machine that you use to take pictures.
कैमरा

camp *noun*
camps

A **camp** is a place where people live in tents for a short time.
शिविर

can *verb*
could

If you **can** do something, you are able to do it.
सकना
I **can** *swim.*

A
B
C
D
E
F
G
H
I
J
K
L
M
N
O
P
Q
R
S
T
U
V
W
X
Y
Z

can *noun*
cans

A **can** is a metal container for food or drink.
कनस्तर
She opened a can of soup.

candle *noun*
candles

A **candle** is a stick of wax with a piece of string through the middle that you burn to give you light.
मोमबत्ती

cannot *verb*

If you **cannot** do something, you are not able to do it.
न कर सकना
I cannot find my bag.

can't

Can't is short for **cannot**.
He can't play the piano.

capital *noun*
capitals

1   The **capital** of a country is the main city, where the country's leaders work.
राजधानी (अंग्रेजी वर्णमाला)
Paris is the capital of France.

2   A **capital** is also a big letter of the alphabet, for example A or R.
बड़ा अक्षर

car *noun*
cars

A **car** is a vehicle with four wheels and an engine that can carry a small number of people.
मोटरगाड़ी

card *noun*
cards

1   **Card** is stiff paper.
गत्ता

2   A **card** is a folded piece of stiff paper that has a picture on the front and a message inside. You send **cards** to people at special times, like birthdays.
बधाई पत्र

3   **Cards** are pieces of stiff paper with numbers or pictures on them that you use for playing games.
ताश

cardboard *noun*

Cardboard is very thick, stiff paper that is used for making boxes.
गत्ता

care *verb*
cares, caring, cared

1   If you **care** about something, you think that it is important.
परवाह करना
He doesn't care about the way he looks.

2   If you **care** for a person or an animal, you look after them.
देखभाल करना
She cared for her pets.

careful *adjective*

If you are **careful**, you think about what you are doing so that you do not make any mistakes.
सावधान
Be careful when you cross the road.

careless *adjective*

If you are **careless**, you do not think about what you are doing, so that you make mistakes.
बेपरवाह
It was careless of me to forget my keys.

carpet *noun*
carpets

A **carpet** is a thick, soft cover for a floor.
कालीन

carpet

carrot *noun*
carrots

A **carrot** is a long, orange vegetable.
गाजर

carry *verb*
carries, carrying, carried

If you **carry** something, you hold it and take it somewhere with you.
ढोना
We carried our bags to the car.

carton noun
cartons

A **carton** is a container made of plastic or cardboard that is used to hold food or drink.
गत्ते का डिब्बा
*I bought a **carton** of milk.*

cartoon noun
cartoons

1 A **cartoon** is a funny drawing.
हास्यचित्र

2 A **cartoon** is also a film that uses drawings, not real people or things.
कार्टून फ़िल्म

case noun
cases

A **case** is a container that is used to hold or carry something.
पेटी
*He put the camera in its **case**.*

castle noun
castles

A **castle** is a large building with very thick, high walls. Most **castles** were built a long time ago to keep the people inside safe from their enemies.
महल

cat noun
cats

A **cat** is an animal that is covered with fur and has a long tail. People often keep small **cats** as pets. Large **cats**, for example lions and tigers, are wild.
बिल्ली

catch verb
catches, catching, caught

1 If you **catch** something that is moving, you take hold of it while it is in the air.
पकड़ना/लपक लेना
*I tried to **catch** the ball.*

2 If you **catch** a bus or a train, you get on it.
पकड़ना
*We **caught** the bus to school.*

3 If you **catch** an illness, you become ill with it.
हो जाना
*He **caught** measles.*

caterpillar noun
caterpillars

A **caterpillar** is a small animal that looks like a worm with lots of short legs. **Caterpillars** turn into butterflies or moths.
इल्ली

cattle noun

Cattle are cows and bulls.
मवेशी
*There were **cattle** in the field.*

caught
⇨ Look at **catch**.
*I jumped and **caught** the ball.*

cauliflower noun
cauliflowers

A **cauliflower** is a big, round, white vegetable with green leaves.
फूलगोभी

cave noun
caves

A **cave** is a big hole in the side of a hill or a mountain, or beneath the ground.
गुफा

CD noun
CDs

CD is short for compact disc.
सी डी
*I bought the band's new **CD**.*

a
b
c
d
e
f
g
h
i
j
k
l
m
n
o
p
q
r
s
t
u
v
w
x
y
z

ceiling *noun*
ceilings

A **ceiling** is the part of a room that is above your head.
छत

centimetre *noun*
centimetres

A **centimetre** is used for measuring the length of something. There are ten millimetres in a **centimetre**, and one hundred **centimetres** in a metre.
सेंटीमीटर

centre *noun*
centres

The **centre** of something is the middle of it.
केंद्र
*She stood in the **centre** of the room.*

cereal *noun*
cereals

1   A **cereal** is a food made from grains that you eat with milk for breakfast.
अनाज

2   A **cereal** is also a kind of plant, for example wheat or rice. The seeds of **cereals** are used for food.
अन्न/धान्य

chain *noun*
chains

A **chain** is a row of rings made of metal that are joined together in a line.
जंज़ीर

chair *noun*
chairs

A **chair** is a seat with a back and four legs, for one person.
कुर्सी
*He suddenly got up from his **chair**.*

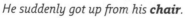

chalk *noun*

Chalk is a kind of soft rock. You use small sticks of **chalk** to write or draw on a blackboard.
चॉक/खड़िया

change *verb*
changes, changing, changed

1   When you **change** something, or when it **changes**, it becomes different.
बदल देना/बदल जाना
*The caterpillar **changed** into a butterfly.*

2   When you **change**, you put on different clothes.
कपड़े बदलना
*He **changed** to go to the party.*

change *noun*

Change is the money that you get back when you pay too much for something.
रेज़गारी

chapter *noun*
chapters

A **chapter** is a part of a book.
अध्याय
*This book has ten **chapters**.*

character *noun*
characters

1   Your **character** is the kind of person you are.
चरित्र

2   A **character** is also a person in a story or a film.
चरित्र/पात्र

charge *verb*
charges, charging, charged

If someone **charges** you an amount of money for something, they ask you to pay that amount for it.
दाम लगाना/दाम मांगना
*They **charged** us too much for our meal.*

chase *verb*
chases, chasing, chased

If you **chase** someone, you run after them and try to catch them.
पीछा करना
*The dog **chased** the cat.*

A B C D E F G H I J K L M N O P Q R S T U V W X Y Z

cheap *adjective*
cheaper, cheapest

If something is **cheap**, you do not have to pay a lot of money for it.
सस्ता
*Milk is very **cheap** in this shop.*

check *verb*
checks, checking, checked

If you **check** something, you make sure that it is right.
जाँचना
*The teacher **checked** my homework.*

cheek *noun*
cheeks

Your **cheeks** are the sides of your face below your eyes.
गाल
*My **cheeks** were red.*

cheer *verb*
cheers, cheering, cheered

When people **cheer**, they shout to show that they like something.
जयजयकार करना
*We all **cheered** when he won the race.*

cheerful *adjective*

Someone who is **cheerful** is happy.
हँसमुख

cheese *noun*

Cheese is a solid food that is made from milk.
पनीर

cheetah *noun*
cheetahs

A **cheetah** is a big wild cat with yellow fur and black spots.
चीता

cherry *noun*
cherries

A **cherry** is a small, round fruit with a hard stone in the middle. **Cherries** are red, black, or yellow.
चेरी

chew *verb*
chews, chewing, chewed

When you **chew** food, you use your teeth to break it up in your mouth before you swallow it.
चबाना

chick *noun*
chicks

A **chick** is a very young bird.
चूजा

chicken *noun*
chickens

1 A **chicken** is a bird that is kept on a farm for its eggs and meat.
मुर्गा/मुर्गी
2 **Chicken** is also the meat that comes from chickens.
मुर्गा/मुर्गी का मांस

child *noun*
children

A **child** is a young boy or girl.
बच्चा

chimney *noun*
chimneys

A **chimney** is a long pipe above a fire. Smoke from the fire goes up the **chimney** and out of the building.
धुआँरा/चिमनी

chimpanzee *noun*
chimpanzees

A **chimpanzee** is a kind of small ape with dark fur.
वनमानुष

a
b
c
d
e
f
g
h
i
j
k
l
m
n
o
p
q
r
s
t
u
v
w
x
y
z

A
B
C
D
E
F
G
H
I
J
K
L
M
N
O
P
Q
R
S
T
U
V
W
X
Y
Z

chin *noun*
chins
Your **chin** is the part of your face below your mouth.
ठोड़ी
*A black beard covered his **chin**.*

chip *noun*
chips
Chips or potato **chips** are thin pieces of potato fried in hot oil.
चिप्स

chip *verb*
chips, chipping, chipped
If you **chip** something, you break a small piece off it by accident.
तोड़ना/किनारे से तोड़ना
*I **chipped** my tooth when I fell.*

chocolate *noun*
chocolates
Chocolate is a sweet brown food that is used to make sweets, cakes, and drinks.
चॉकलेट

choose *verb*
chooses, choosing, chose, chosen
If you **choose** something, you decide to have it.
चुनना
*You can **choose** any book you want.*

chop *verb*
chops, chopping, chopped
If you **chop** something, you cut it into pieces with a knife or an axe.
टुकड़ा करना
*He **chopped** some wood for the fire.*

chose
⇨ Look at **choose**.
*She **chose** a dress to wear.*

chosen
⇨ Look at **choose**.
*We have **chosen** which film to watch.*

circle *noun*
circles
A **circle** is a round shape.
वृत्त/गोला

circus *noun*
circuses
A **circus** is a big tent where you go to see clowns and animals.
सर्कस

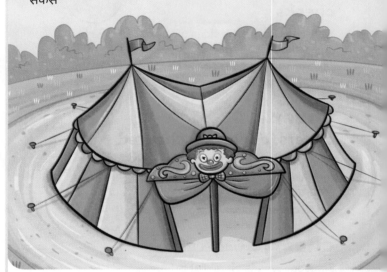

city *noun*
cities
A **city** is a very big town where a lot of people live and work.
नगर/शहर

clap *verb*
claps, clapping, clapped
When you **clap**, you hit your hands together to make a loud noise. People **clap** to show that they like something.
ताली बजाना
*Everyone **clapped** at the end of her song.*

class *noun*
classes
A **class** is a group of people who are taught together.
कक्षा
*He is in my **class** at school.*

classroom *noun*
classrooms

A **classroom** is a room in a school where children have lessons.
कक्षा

claw *noun*
claws

A bird's or an animal's **claws** are the hard, sharp, curved parts at the end of its feet.
पंजा

clean *adjective*
cleaner, cleanest

Something that is **clean** does not have any dirt or marks on it.
साफ़
*Make sure your hands are **clean**.*

clean *verb*
cleans, cleaning, cleaned

When you **clean** something, you take all the dirt off it.
साफ़ करना
*I **clean** my teeth before bedtime.*

clear *adjective*
clearer, clearest

1 If something is **clear**, it is easy to understand, to see, or to hear.
स्पष्ट
*He gave us **clear** instructions on what to do.*

2 If something like glass or plastic is **clear**, you can see through it.
साफ़/निर्मल
*The bottle was full of a **clear** liquid.*

3 If a place is **clear**, it does not have anything there that you do not want.
खाली
*You can cross the road when it is **clear**.*

clear *verb*
clears, clearing, cleared

When you **clear** a place, you take away all the things you do not want there.
साफ़-सुथरा करना
*She **cleared** the table.*

clever *adjective*
cleverer, cleverest

Someone who is **clever** can learn and understand things quickly.
चतुर/चालाक
*She is very **clever** at maths.*

cliff *noun*
cliffs

A **cliff** is a hill with one side that is very steep. **Cliffs** are often beside the sea.
खड़ी चट्टान

climb *verb*
climbs, climbing, climbed

If you **climb** something, you move towards the top of it. You sometimes use your hands as well as your feet when you **climb**.
चढ़ना
*We **climbed** the tree in the garden.*

cloak *noun*
cloaks

A **cloak** is a very loose coat without sleeves.
लबादा/चोगा

clock *noun*
clocks

A **clock** is a machine that shows you the time.
दीवार घड़ी

close *verb*
closes, closing, closed

When you **close** something, you shut it.
बंद करना
*Please **close** the door behind you.*

close *adjective*
closer, closest

If something is **close** to another thing, it is near it.
समीप/पास
*Our house is **close** to the park.*

cloth *noun*
cloths

1 **Cloth** is material that is used to make things like clothes and curtains.
कपड़ा/वस्त्र

2 A **cloth** is a piece of material that you use to clean something.
पोंछा

clothes *noun*

Clothes are the things that people wear, for example shirts, trousers, and dresses.
पोशाक

cloud *noun*
clouds

A **cloud** is a white or grey shape that you see in the sky. **Clouds** are made of tiny drops of water that sometimes turn into rain.
मेघ/बादल

clown *noun*
clowns

A **clown** is a person who wears funny clothes and does silly things to make people laugh.
मसखरा, जोकर

coat *noun*
coats

You wear a **coat** on top of your other clothes when you go outside.
कोट

cobweb *noun*
cobwebs

A **cobweb** is a very thin net that a spider makes to catch insects.
मकड़ी का जाला

coconut *noun*
coconuts

A **coconut** is a very large nut that has a very hard shell and is white inside. **Coconuts** are full of a liquid called **coconut** milk.
नारियल

coffee *noun*

Coffee is a drink. You make it by pouring hot water on **coffee** beans.
कॉफ़ी
*Coffee beans grow on a **coffee** plant.*

coin *noun*
coins

A **coin** is a round, flat piece of metal that is used as money.
सिक्का

cold *adjective*
colder, coldest

1 If you are **cold**, you do not feel comfortable because you are not warm enough.
ठंडा/सर्द
*Wear a jumper if you are **cold**.*

2 If something is **cold**, it is not hot.
ठंडा/सर्द
*The weather is very **cold**.*

cold *noun*
colds

When you have a **cold**, you sneeze and cough a lot, and you have a sore throat.
ज़ुकाम

collar *noun*
collars

1 The **collar** of a shirt or jacket is the part that goes around your neck.
गिरेबान/कॉलर

2 A **collar** is also a band that goes around the neck of a dog or cat.
गले का पट्टा

collect _verb_
collects, collecting, collected

1 If you **collect** things, you bring them together.
इकट्ठा करना
He **collected** wood for the fire.

2 If you **collect** someone from a place, you go there and take them away.
ले आना
Mum **collected** us from school.

colour _noun_
colours

Red, blue and yellow are the main **colours**. You can mix them together to make other **colours**.
रंग

comb _noun_
combs

A **comb** is a flat piece of metal or plastic with very thin points that you use to make your hair tidy.
कंघी

come _verb_
comes, coming, came, come

When you **come** to a place, you move towards it or arrive there.
आना
She **came** into the room.

comfortable _adjective_

If something is **comfortable**, it makes you feel good.
आरामदेह/सुविधाजनक
This is a very **comfortable** chair.

comic _noun_
comics

A **comic** is a magazine with stories that are told in pictures.
चित्रकथा

common _adjective_

If things are **common**, you see lots of them around, or they happen often.
सामान्य/एक समान
Foxes are quite **common** in this area.

compact disc _noun_
compact discs

A **compact disc** is a round, flat piece of plastic that has music or information on it. **Compact discs** are also called CDs.
कॉम्पैक्ट डिस्क

competition _noun_
competitions

When you are in a **competition**, you try to show that you are the best at something.
प्रतिस्पर्धा/प्रतियोगिता
She won the painting **competition**.

complete _adjective_

If something is **complete**, none of it is missing.
पूर्ण/पूरा
He had a **complete** set of crayons.

computer _noun_
computers

A **computer** is a machine that can store a lot of information and can work things out very quickly.
कंप्यूटर/संगणक
We played games on our **computer**.

confused _adjective_

If you are **confused**, you do not understand what is happening, or you do not know what to do.
चकराया हुआ
She was **confused** about where to go.

consonant _noun_
consonants

A **consonant** is any letter of the alphabet that is not a, e, i, o, or u.
व्यंजन
The word "book" has two **consonants** in it.

container _noun_
containers

A **container** is something that you use to keep things in, for example a box or a bottle.
डिब्बा

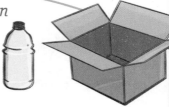

a
b
c
d
e
f
g
h
i
j
k
l
m
n
o
p
q
r
s
t
u
v
w
x
y
z

A
B
C
D
E
F
G
H
I
J
K
L
M
N
O
P
Q
R
S
T
U
V
W
X
Y
Z

control *verb*
controls, controlling, controlled

If you **control** something, you can make it do what you want.
नियंत्रित करना
*I can **control** the speed by pressing this button.*

cook *verb*
cooks, cooking, cooked

When you **cook** food, you make it hot and get it ready to eat.
खाना पकाना
*Mum was **cooking** dinner.*

cooker *noun*
cookers

A **cooker** is a machine that you use to cook food.
कुकर

cool *adjective*
cooler, coolest

Something that is **cool** is quite cold.
शीतल/ठंडा
*Put the milk in the fridge to keep it **cool**.*

copy *noun*
copies

A **copy** is something that is made to look like another thing.
प्रति/प्रतिरूप
*I made a **copy** of the drawing.*

corn *noun*

Corn is a long vegetable. It is covered with yellow seeds that you eat.
मकई

corner *noun*
corners

A **corner** is a place where two sides join together.
कोना
*He stood at the **corner** of the street.*

correct *adjective*

If something is **correct**, there are no mistakes in it.
सही/ठीक

cost *noun*
costs

The **cost** of something is the amount of money you need to buy it.
लागत/कीमत
*The **cost** of the holiday was too high.*

cot *noun*
cots

A **cot** is a bed for a baby, with high sides to stop the baby from falling out.
पालना

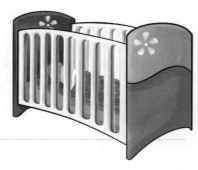

cotton *noun*

1 **Cotton** is a kind of cloth that is made from the **cotton** plant.
सूती कपड़ा

2 **Cotton** is also thread that you use to sew with.
धागा/रूई या कपास

cough *verb*
coughs, coughing, coughed

When you **cough**, you make air come out of your throat with a sudden, loud noise.
खाँसना
*The smoke made us **cough**.*

could *verb*

If you say you **could** do something, you mean that you were able to do it. **Could** comes from the word **can**.
सकना
*I **could** see through the window.*

couldn't

Couldn't is short for **could not**.
न कर सकना
*She **couldn't** open the door.*

count verb
counts, counting, counted

1 When you **count**, you say numbers in order, one after the other.
गिनना

I counted from one to ten.

2 When you **count** all the things in a group, you add them up to see how many there are.
गिनती करना

The teacher counted the children in the class.

country noun
countries

1 A **country** is a part of the world with its own people and laws.
देश

He lives in a different country.

2 The **country** is land that is away from towns and cities. There are farms and woods in the **country**.
देहात/गाँव

We went for a walk in the country.

cousin noun
cousins

Your **cousin** is the son or daughter of your uncle or aunt.
चचेरा/ममेरा/फुफेरा/मौसेरा/ भाई या बहन

cover verb
covers, covering, covered

If you **cover** something, you put another thing over it.
ढँकना

She covered the table with a cloth.

cover noun
covers

A **cover** is something that you put over another thing.
खोल/गिलाफ़

Put a cover over the sofa to keep it clean.

cow noun
cows

A **cow** is a large animal that is kept on farms because it gives milk.
गाय

crab noun
crabs

A **crab** is an animal with a hard shell that lives in the sea. **Crabs** have large claws on their front legs.
केकड़ा

crack verb
cracks, cracking, cracked

If something **cracks**, it becomes damaged, and lines appear on the surface where it has broken.
चिटकना

The window cracked.

crane noun
cranes

1 A **crane** is a tall machine that can lift very heavy things.
भारी सामान उठाने की मशीन

2 A **crane** is also a large bird with a long neck and long legs. **Cranes** live near water.
सारस

crash noun
crashes

1 A **crash** is an accident when a vehicle hits something.
टक्कर/दुर्घटना

There was a car crash outside the school.

2 A **crash** is also a sudden, loud noise.
धड़ाका/धमाका

He dropped the plates with a crash.

crawl verb
crawls, crawling, crawled

When you **crawl**, you move along on your hands and knees.
रेंगना

The baby crawled along the floor.

crayon noun
crayons

Crayons are pencils or sticks of wax in different colours that you use for drawing.
मोम वाले रंग

cream noun

Cream is a thick liquid that is made from milk. You can use it in cooking or pour it over puddings.
मलाई/क्रीम

a
b
c
d
e
f
g
h
i
j
k
l
m
n
o
p
q
r
s
t
u
v
w
x
y
z

31

creature noun
creatures

A **creature** is anything that is alive, but is not a plant.
प्राणी
*Many **creatures** live in the forest.*

creep verb
creeps, creeping, crept

1 If you **creep** somewhere, you move in a very slow and quiet way.
दबे पाँव चलना
*He **crept** up the stairs.*

2 If an animal **creeps**, it moves along close to the ground.
रेंगना
*The mouse **crept** across the room.*

crew noun
crews

A **crew** is a group of people who work together on a ship or an aeroplane.
कर्मचारी दल

cricket noun
crickets

1 **Cricket** is a game where two teams take turns to hit a ball with a bat and run up and down.
क्रिकेट

2 A **cricket** is also a small jumping insect that rubs its wings together to make a high sound.
झींगुर

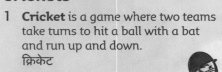

cried
⇨ Look at **cry**.
*The baby **cried** for its mother.*

cries
⇨ Look at **cry**.
*She always **cries** at sad films.*

crocodile noun
crocodiles

A **crocodile** is a large reptile with a long body, a long mouth and sharp teeth. **Crocodiles'** mouths are in the shape of a letter V.
मगरमच्छ

crop noun
crops

Crops are plants that people grow for food, for example potatoes and wheat.
फसल

cross verb
crosses, crossing, crossed

If you **cross** something, you go from one side of it to the other.
पार करना
Cross the road where it is safe.

cross noun
crosses

A **cross** is a mark that you write. It looks like ×.
काटने का चिह्न लगाना
*She put a **cross** beside my name.*

cross adjective
crosser, crossest

If you are **cross**, you feel angry about something.
अप्रसन्न
*Mum was **cross** because we were late.*

crowd noun
crowds

A **crowd** is a lot of people together in one place.
भीड़
*A big **crowd** came to see the game.*

crown noun
crowns

A **crown** is a circle made of gold or silver and jewels that kings and queens wear on their heads.
मुकुट/ताज

cry verb
cries, crying, cried

When you **cry**, tears come from your eyes. People **cry** when they are sad or hurt.
रोना
*The baby started to **cry**.*

cry noun
cries

A **cry** is a loud sound that you make with your voice.
चिल्लाना
*I heard the **cry** of a bird.*

cub noun
cubs

A **cub** is a young wild animal, for example a young bear or lion.
शावक

cube noun
cubes

A **cube** is a solid shape with six sides that are all squares.
घन
*A dice is in the shape of a **cube**.*

cucumber noun
cucumbers

A **cucumber** is a long, thin, green vegetable that you eat in salads.
खीरा

cuddle verb
cuddles, cuddling, cuddled

If you **cuddle** someone, you put your arms around them and hold them close to you.
लिपटाना

cup noun
cups

A **cup** is a small, round container with a handle. You drink things like tea and coffee from a **cup**.
प्याला

cupboard noun
cupboards

A **cupboard** is a piece of furniture with a door and shelves that you keep things in.
अलमारी
*The **cupboard** was full of toys.*

curl noun
curls

A **curl** is a piece of hair that has a curved shape.
घूँघर/छल्ला
*The girl had long, black **curls**.*

curtain noun
curtains

A **curtain** is a piece of cloth that you pull across a window to cover it.
परदा

curved adjective

If something is **curved**, it has the shape of a bent line.
वक्र/मुड़ा हुआ
*The bird had a **curved** beak.*

cushion noun
cushions

A **cushion** is a bag of soft material that you put on a seat to make it more comfortable.
गद्दी

customer noun
customers

A **customer** is a person who buys something in a shop.
ग्राहक

cut verb
cuts, cutting, cut

1 If you **cut** something, you use a knife or scissors to divide it into pieces.
काटना
*We **cut** the cake.*

2 If you **cut** yourself, something sharp goes through your skin and blood comes out.
काट लेना (घाव लगाने के अर्थ में)
*Don't **cut** yourself on the broken glass.*

cut noun
cuts

A **cut** is a place on your skin where something sharp has gone through it.
घाव/चीरा
*He had a **cut** on his cheek.*

a
b
c
d
e
f
g
h
i
j
k
l
m
n
o
p
q
r
s
t
u
v
w
x
y
z

dad or daddy noun
dads or **daddies**

Dad or **daddy** is a name for your father.
पिता

damage verb
damages, damaging, damaged

If you **damage** something, you break it or spoil it.
क्षति पहुँचाना
*The storm **damaged** the roof.*

damp adjective
damper, dampest

Something that is **damp** is a little bit wet.
नम
*Her hair was **damp**.*

dance verb
dances, dancing, danced

When you **dance**, you move your body to music.
नृत्य करना

danger noun
dangers

If there is **danger**, something bad might happen to hurt you.
खतरा
*There is a **danger** that he will fall.*

dangerous adjective

If something is **dangerous**, it can hurt you or kill you.
खतरनाक
*It is **dangerous** to cross the road here.*

dark adjective
darker, darkest

1 When it is **dark**, there is no light or not much light.
अँधेरा

2 A **dark** colour is not pale.
गहरा रंग
*She wore a **dark** blue skirt.*

date noun
dates

A **date** is the day, the month, and sometimes the year when something happens.
दिनांक/तिथि
*What **date** is your birthday?*

daughter noun
daughters

Someone's **daughter** is their female child.
पुत्री/बेटी

day noun
days

1 A **day** is the length of time between one midnight and the next. There are twenty-four hours in a **day**, and seven **days** in a week.
दिन
*It is three **days** until my birthday.*

2 **Day** is the time when there is light outside.
दिन का समय
*I've been busy all **day**.*

dead adjective

A person, an animal, or a plant that is **dead** has stopped living.
मृत/मरा हुआ

deaf adjective

Someone who is **deaf** cannot hear anything, or cannot hear very well.
बहरा

December noun

December is the month after November and before January. It has 31 days.
दिसंबर

decide *verb*
decides, deciding, decided
When you **decide** to do something, you think about it and then choose to do it.
निश्चय करना
*She **decided** to go home.*

decorate *verb*
decorates, decorating, decorated
If you **decorate** a room, you put paint or paper on its walls.
सजाना
*We **decorated** the bedroom.*

deep *adjective*
deeper, deepest
If something is **deep**, it goes down a long way.
गहरा
*We dug a **deep** hole in the sand.*

deer *noun*
deer
A **deer** is a large animal that lives in forests and can run very fast. Male **deer** have big horns that look like branches on their heads.
हिरन

defend *verb*
defends, defending, defended
If you **defend** someone, you keep them safe from danger.
रक्षा करना
*The soldiers **defended** the king.*

delicious *adjective*
If food is **delicious**, it tastes or smells very good.
स्वादिष्ट

deliver *verb*
delivers, delivering, delivered
If you **deliver** something, you take it to someone.
पहुँचाना
*Please **deliver** this letter to him.*

dentist *noun*
dentists
A **dentist** is a person whose job is to take care of people's teeth.
दंत चिकित्सक

depth *noun*
depths
The **depth** of something is how far down it goes from its top to its bottom.
गहराई
*The **depth** of the pond is two metres.*

describe *verb*
describes, describing, described
If you **describe** something, you say what it is like.
वर्णन करना
*He **described** the picture to me.*

desert *noun*
deserts
A **desert** is a large, dry area of land with almost no trees or plants. **Deserts** are very hot and are often covered with sand.
रेगिस्तान

desk *noun*
desks
A **desk** is a kind of table that you sit at to write or to work.
मेज़

destroy *verb*
destroys, destroying, destroyed
If you **destroy** something, you damage it so much that it cannot be used any more.
नष्ट करना
*The fire **destroyed** the house.*

a
b
c
d
e
f
g
h
i
j
k
l
m
n
o
p
q
r
s
t
u
v
w
x
y
z

35

A
B
C
D
E
F
G
H
I
J
K
L
M
N
O
P
Q
R
S
T
U
V
W
X
Y
Z

diagram noun
diagrams

A **diagram** is a drawing that shows something in a way that is very easy to understand.
चित्र
*He drew me a **diagram** of the engine.*

diamond noun
diamonds

1 A **diamond** is a kind of jewel that is hard, clear, and shiny.
हीरा

2 A **diamond** is also a shape with four straight sides.
विषमकोणीय समचतुर्भुज

diary noun
diaries

A **diary** is a book that you use to write down things that happen to you each day.
रोजनामचा

dice noun
dice

A **dice** is a small cube with a different number of spots on each side. You throw **dice** in some games.
पासा

dictionary noun
dictionaries

A **dictionary** is a book with a list of words in it. The **dictionary** tells you what these words mean, and shows you how to spell them.
शब्दकोश

did
⇨ Look at **do**.
*I saw what you **did**.*

didn't

Didn't is short for **did not**.
नहीं किया
*She **didn't** like the film.*

die verb
dies, dying, died

When a person, an animal, or a plant **dies**, they stop living.
मरना
*Plants **die** if you don't water them.*

different adjective

If two things are **different**, they are not like each other.
अलग
*The crayons were all in **different** colours.*

difficult adjective

If something is **difficult**, it is not easy to do or to understand.
कठिन
*The homework was too **difficult** for us.*

dig verb
digs, digging, dug

If you **dig**, you make a hole in the ground.
खोदना
*We **dug** a hole in the garden.*

digital adjective

If a machine is **digital**, it shows or sends information by using numbers.
डिजिटल
*We have a new **digital** television.*

dinner noun
dinners

Dinner is the main meal of the day.
रात का भोजन

dinosaur *noun*
dinosaurs

Dinosaurs were large animals that lived a very long time ago. **Dinosaurs** were like very big lizards.
डायनासोर

direction *noun*
directions

1 A **direction** is the way that you go to get to a place.
दिशा/ओर
My house is in this direction.

2 **Directions** are words or pictures that show you how to do something, or how to get somewhere.
निर्देश
He gave me directions to the station.

dirt *noun*

Dirt is anything that is not clean, for example, dust or mud.
गंदगी
She had dirt on her face.

dirty *adjective*
dirtier, dirtiest

If something is **dirty**, it has mud, food, or other marks on it.
गंदा
The dishes were dirty.

disappear *verb*
disappears, disappearing, disappeared

If something **disappears**, you cannot see it any more.
गायब होना
The cat disappeared under the bed.

disappointed *adjective*

If you are **disappointed**, you are sad because something you hoped for did not happen.
निराश
I was disappointed that you weren't there.

disaster *noun*
disasters

A **disaster** is something very bad that happens suddenly and that may hurt many people.
तबाही

discover *verb*
discovers, discovering, discovered

When you **discover** something, you get to know about it for the first time.
पता लगाना/खोज करना
We discovered that he was very good at football.

discuss *verb*
discusses, discussing, discussed

When people **discuss** something, they talk about it together.
चर्चा करना
We discussed what to do next.

disease *noun*
diseases

A **disease** is something that makes you ill.
बीमारी/रोग
Measles is a disease.

disguise *noun*
disguises

A **disguise** is something you wear so that people will not know who you are.
भेष बदलना

dish *noun*
dishes

A **dish** is a container that you use to cook or serve food in.
थाली

disk *noun*
disks

A **disk** is a flat piece of metal and plastic that you use in a computer to store information.
डिस्क

a
b
c
d
e
f
g
h
i
j
k
l
m
n
o
p
q
r
s
t
u
v
w
x
y
z

A
B
C
D
E
F
G
H
I
J
K
L
M
N
O
P
Q
R
S
T
U
V
W
X
Y
Z

distance *noun*
distances

The **distance** between two things is how much space there is between them.

दूरी

*Measure the **distance** between the wall and the table.*

dive *verb*
dives, diving, dived

If you **dive** into water, you jump in so that your arms and your head go in first.

डुबकी लगाना/गोता लगाना

divide *verb*
divides, dividing, divided

1   If you **divide** something, you make it into smaller pieces.
    विभाजित करना
    ***Divide** the cake into four pieces.*

2   When you **divide** numbers, you see how many times one number goes into another number.
    भाग देना
    *If you **divide** ten by five, you get two.*

do *verb*
does, doing, did, done

If you **do** something, you spend some time on it or finish it.

करना

*I tried to **do** some work.*

doctor *noun*
doctors

A **doctor** is a person whose job is to help people who are ill or hurt to get better.

चिकित्सक

does

⇨ Look at **do**.
*She **does** her homework before dinner.*

doesn't

Doesn't is short for **does not**.
नहीं करता है
*He **doesn't** like carrots.*

dog *noun*
dogs

A **dog** is an animal that barks. Some **dogs** do special jobs, like helping blind people.
कुत्ता

doing

⇨ Look at **do**.
*What are you **doing**?*

doll *noun*
dolls

A **doll** is a toy that looks like a small person or a baby.
गुड़िया

dolphin *noun*
dolphins

A **dolphin** is an animal that lives in the sea and looks like a large fish with a long nose. **Dolphins** are very clever.
डॉल्फ़िन

done

⇨ Look at **do**.
*She has **done** a drawing.*

donkey *noun*
donkeys

A **donkey** is an animal that looks like a small horse with long ears.
गधा

38

don't

Don't is short for **do not**.
नहीं करना
I **don't** feel well.

door noun
doors

You open and close a **door** to get
into a building, a room, or a cupboard.
दरवाज़ा

double adjective

Double means two times as big, or two times
as much.
दोगुना
His room is **double** the size of mine.

down

When something moves **down**, it goes from a higher
place to a lower place.
नीचे की ओर
She came **down** the stairs.

drag verb
drags, dragging, dragged

If you **drag** something, you pull it along the ground.
घसीटना
He **dragged** his chair to the table.

dragon noun
dragons

In stories, a **dragon** is a
monster that has wings
and can make fire come
out of its mouth.
ड्रैगन - एक काल्पनिक प्राणी

drain verb
drains, draining, drained

If you **drain** a liquid, you take it away by making it
flow to another place.
बहाना
They **drained** the water out of the tunnel.

drank

⇨ Look at **drink**.
She **drank** a bottle of water.

draw verb
draws, drawing, drew, drawn

When you **draw**, you use pens, pencils, or crayons to
make a picture.
अंकित करना/चित्र बनाना
He likes to **draw** animals.

drawer noun
drawers

A **drawer** is a box that fits inside a piece of furniture.
You can pull it out and put things in it.
दराज

drawing noun
drawings

A **drawing** is a picture you make with
pens, pencils, or crayons.
रेखाचित्र

drawn

⇨ Look at **draw**.
I have **drawn** my house.

dream noun
dreams

A **dream** is something you see
and hear in your mind while you
are sleeping.
सपना
I had a **dream** about winning the prize.

dress noun
dresses

A **dress** is something a girl or a woman
can wear. It covers the body and part
of the legs.
पोशाक
She wore a yellow **dress**.

a
b
c
d
e
f
g
h
i
j
k
l
m
n
o
p
q
r
s
t
u
v
w
x
y
z

A
B
C
D
E
F
G
H
I
J
K
L
M
N
O
P
Q
R
S
T
U
V
W
X
Y
Z

dress *verb*
dresses, dressing, dressed

When you **dress**, you put on clothes.
कपड़े पहनना
*He **dressed** quickly because he was late.*

drew
⇨ Look at **draw**.
*She **drew** a picture of a horse.*

drink *verb*
drinks, drinking, drank, drunk

When you **drink**, you swallow liquid.
पीना
*Mum **drinks** a lot of coffee.*

drip *verb*
drips, dripping, dripped

When liquid **drips**, a small amount of it falls from somewhere.
टपकना
*Water **dripped** from the roof.*

drive *verb*
drives, driving, drove, driven

When someone **drives** a vehicle, they make it go where they want.
गाड़ी चलाना
*He knows how to **drive** a car.*

drop *verb*
drops, dropping, dropped

If you **drop** something, you let it fall.
गिराना
*I **dropped** a plate on the floor.*

drove
⇨ Look at **drive**.
*We **drove** to the shops.*

drown *verb*
drowns, drowning, drowned

If someone **drowns**, they die because their face is below water and they cannot breathe.
डूबना

drum *noun*
drums

A **drum** is an instrument that you hit with sticks or with your hands to make music.
ढोल

drunk
⇨ Look at **drink**.
*Have you **drunk** all the milk?*

dry *adjective*
drier, driest

If something is **dry**, there is no water in it or on it.
सूखा हुआ/शुष्क
*My clothes are **dry**.*

duck *noun*
ducks

A **duck** is a bird that lives near water and can swim. **Ducks** have large flat beaks.
बत्तख

dug
⇨ Look at **dig**.
*We **dug** a hole in the sand.*

dull *adjective*
duller, dullest

1 Something that is **dull** is not interesting.
नीरस
*That was a very **dull** book.*

2 A **dull** colour is not bright.
फीका
*He wore a **dull** green jacket.*

dust *noun*

Dust is tiny pieces of dry dirt that looks like powder.
धूल
*The table was covered in **dust**.*

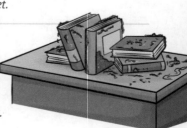

Ee

each

Each means every one.
प्रत्येक
*He gave **each** of us a book.*

eagle *noun*
eagles

An **eagle** is a large bird
with a curved beak and sharp
claws. **Eagles** eat small animals.
चील

ear *noun*
ears

Your **ears** are the two parts of your body that you hear
sounds with.
कान
*He whispered something in her **ear**.*

early *adjective*
earlier, earliest

1   If you are **early**, you arrive before the time that
    you were expected to come.
    जल्दी/समय से पूर्व
    *She was too **early** for the party.*

2   **Early** also means near the first part of something.
    जल्दी
    *I got up **early** in the morning.*

earn *verb*
earns, earning, earned

If you **earn** money, you work to get it.
कमाना
*He **earned** some money washing the car.*

earth *noun*

1   The **Earth** is the planet
    that we live on.
    पृथ्वी

2   **Earth** is also the soil
    that plants grow in.
    मिट्टी/भूमि

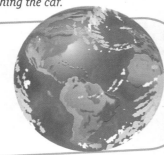

earthquake *noun*
earthquakes

When there is an **earthquake**, the ground shakes
and buildings often fall down.
भूकंप

east *noun*

The **east** is the
direction that is in
front of you when
you are looking
towards the place
where the sun rises.
पूरब/पूर्व

easy *adjective*
easier, easiest

If something is **easy**, you can do it or understand it
without having to try very much.
आसान
*These sums are **easy**.*

eat *verb*
eats, eating, ate, eaten

When you **eat**, you chew and swallow food.
खाना
*She **eats** too many sweets.*

echo *noun*
echoes

An **echo** is a sound that you hear again because it
bounces off something solid and then comes back.
प्रतिध्वनि/गूँज
*We heard the **echo** of our voices in the cave.*

a
b
c
d
e
f
g
h
i
j
k
l
m
n
o
p
q
r
s
t
u
v
w
x
y
z

A
B
C
D
E
F
G
H
I
J
K
L
M
N
O
P
Q
R
S
T
U
V
W
X
Y
Z

edge *noun*
edges

The **edge** of something is the part along the end or side of it.
किनारा

*She stood at the **edge** of the pond.*

effect *noun*
effects

An **effect** is something that happens because of another thing.
प्रभाव

*The flood was an **effect** of all the rain.*

effort *noun*
efforts

If you make an **effort** to do something, you have to work a lot to do it.
प्रयास

*She made an **effort** to win the race.*

egg *noun*
eggs

Baby birds, insects, and some other animals live in **eggs** until they are big enough to come out and be born. People often eat hens' **eggs** as food.
अंडा

eight *noun*

Eight is the number 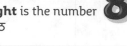 8.
आठ

elbow *noun*
elbows

Your **elbow** is the part in the middle of your arm where it bends.
कोहनी

*She put her **elbows** on the table.*

electricity *noun*

Electricity is a kind of energy that is used to make light, to make things hot, and to make machines work.
बिजली

elephant *noun*
elephants

An **elephant** is a very large, grey animal with big ears, a long nose called a trunk, and two long, curved teeth called tusks.
हाथी

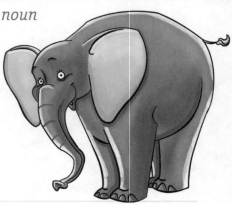

eleven *noun*

Eleven is the number **11**.
ग्यारह

email or e-mail *noun*

An **email** is a message like a letter that you send from one computer to another.
ई-मेल

*I got an **email** from my cousin.*

empty *adjective*
emptier, emptiest

If something is **empty**, there is nothing inside it.
खाली

*The bottle was **empty**.*

encyclopedia *noun*
encyclopedias

An **encyclopedia** is a book that gives you information about many different things.
विश्वकोश

end *noun*
ends

The **end** of something is the last part of it.
अंत

*He told me the **end** of the story.*

enemy *noun*
enemies

If someone is your **enemy**, they hate you and want to hurt you.
शत्रु

energy *noun*

1 If you have **energy**, you have the strength to move around a lot and do things.
ऊर्जा
*He has the **energy** to run for miles.*

2 **Energy** is also the power that makes machines work.
ऊर्जा
*The lamp gets its **energy** from the sun.*

engine *noun*
engines

1 An **engine** is a machine that makes things like cars and planes move.
इंजन

2 An **engine** is also the front part of a train that pulls it along.
इंजन

enjoy *verb*
enjoys, enjoying, enjoyed

If you **enjoy** something, you like doing it.
आनंद उठाना
*I **enjoy** reading.*

enormous *adjective*

Something that is **enormous** is very big.
विशाल
*Whales are **enormous**.*

enough

If you have **enough** of something, you have as much as you need.
पर्याप्त/काफी
*I don't have **enough** money to buy both books.*

enter *verb*
enters, entering, entered

When you **enter** a place, you go into it.
प्रवेश करना

entrance *noun*
entrances

The **entrance** of a place is the way you get into it.
प्रवेश
*We found the **entrance** to the tunnel.*

envelope *noun*
envelopes

An **envelope** is a paper cover that you put a letter or a card into before you send it to someone.
लिफ़ाफ़ा

environment *noun*

The **environment** is the land, water, and air around us.
पर्यावरण
*We must try to protect the **environment**.*

equal *adjective*

If two things are **equal**, they are the same in size, number, or amount.
समतुल्य/बराबर
*Mix **equal** amounts of milk and water.*

equipment *noun*

Equipment is all the things that you need to do something.
उपकरण
*He put his football **equipment** in his bag.*

escape *verb*
escapes, escaping, escaped

If a person or an animal **escapes**, they get away from somewhere.
पलायन करना/छूट निकलना
*My guinea pig **escaped** from its cage.*

even *adjective*

1 An **even** number is a number that you can divide by two, with nothing left over.
सम संख्या
*Four is an **even** number.*

2 Something that is **even** is flat and smooth.
समतल
*The path was straight and **even**.*

a
b
c
d
e
f
g
h
i
j
k
l
m
n
o
p
q
r
s
t
u
v
w
x
y
z

A
B
C
D
E
F
G
H
I
J
K
L
M
N
O
P
Q
R
S
T
U
V
W
X
Y
Z

evening *noun*
evenings

The **evening** is the part of each day between the end of the afternoon and the time when people usually go to bed.
शाम/सायं

ever

Ever means at any time.
कदापि
*Have you **ever** seen anything like it?*

every *adjective*

You use **every** to mean all the people or things in a group.
प्रत्येक
Every pupil in the school was there.

everybody

Everybody means all the people in a group, or all the people in the world.
प्रत्येक व्यक्ति
Everybody likes him.

everyone

Everyone means all the people in a group, or all the people in the world.
हर कोई
Everyone knows who she is.

everything

Everything means all of something.
सब कुछ
*He told me **everything** that happened.*

everywhere

Everywhere means in every place.
सर्वत्र
*I looked **everywhere** for my keys.*

example *noun*
examples

An **example** is something that you use to show what other things in the same group are like.
उदाहरण
*Here is an **example** of my drawings.*

excellent *adjective*

Something that is **excellent** is very good.
उत्तम
*It was an **excellent** film.*

excited *adjective*

If you are **excited**, you are very happy about something and you keep thinking about it.
उत्तेजित
*He was very **excited** about going to the beach.*

excuse *noun*
excuses

An **excuse** is a reason that you give to explain why you did something.
बहाना
*She had a good **excuse** for being late.*

exercise *noun*
exercises

1   When you do **exercise**, you move your body so that you can keep healthy and strong.
व्यायाम
*Running and swimming are both good **exercise**.*

2   An **exercise** is also something you do to practise what you have learnt.
अभ्यास
*We did a maths **exercise**.*

exit *noun*
exits

The **exit** of a building is the door you use to get out of it.
प्रस्थान/बाहर जाने का मार्ग
*We left by the nearest **exit**.*

expect *verb*
expects, expecting, expected

If you **expect** something to happen, you think that it will happen.
आशा करना
*I **expect** that he will come.*

expensive *adjective*

If something is **expensive**, you need a lot of money to buy it.
महंगा

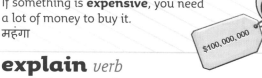

$100,000,000

explain *verb*
explains, explaining, explained

If you **explain** something, you talk about it so that people can understand it.
व्याख्या करना
*He **explained** to me how the machine worked.*

explode *verb*
explodes, exploding, exploded

If something **explodes**, it bursts with a very loud noise.
विस्फोटित होना

explore *verb*
explores, exploring, explored

If you **explore** a place, you look around it to see what it is like.
पता लगाना
*We **explored** the old castle.*

extinct *adjective*

If an animal or a plant is **extinct**, there are none of them alive any more.
विलुप्त
*Dinosaurs are **extinct**.*

extra *adjective*

Extra means more than the usual amount.
अतिरिक्त
*I wore an **extra** jumper because it was cold.*

eye *noun*
eyes

Your **eyes** are the parts of your body that you see with.
आँख
*I opened my **eyes** and looked.*

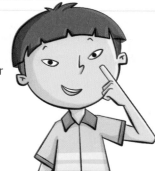

face *noun*
faces

Your **face** is the front part of your head.
चेहरा
*She has a beautiful **face**.*

fact *noun*
facts

A **fact** is something that you know is true.
तथ्य

factory *noun*
factories

A **factory** is a large building where people use machines to make things.
कारखाना
*He works in a **factory** that makes computers.*

fail *verb*
fails, failing, failed

If you **fail**, you try to do something but you cannot do it.
असफल होना
*She **failed** to find her lost keys.*

fair *adjective*
fairer, fairest

1 If something is **fair**, it seems right because it is the same for everyone.
उचित
*It's not **fair** – he's got more than me!*

2 **Fair** hair is pale yellow in colour.
हल्का पीला/गोरा

a
b
c
d
e
f
g
h
i
j
k
l
m
n
o
p
q
r
s
t
u
v
w
x
y
z

A
B
C
D
E
F
G
H
I
J
K
L
M
N
O
P
Q
R
S
T
U
V
W
X
Y
Z

fairy noun
fairies

In stories, **fairies** are tiny creatures with wings who can do magic.
परी

fall verb
falls, falling, fell, fallen

If a person or thing **falls**, they move towards the ground suddenly by accident.
गिरना
*He **fell** off his bike.*

fallen

⇨ Look at **fall**.
*An apple had **fallen** from the tree.*

family noun
families

A **family** is a group of people made up of parents and their children. Aunts and uncles, cousins, grandmothers, and grandfathers are also part of your **family**.
परिवार

famous adjective

If someone is **famous**, a lot of people know who they are.
प्रसिद्ध
*She wants to be rich and **famous**.*

far
farther, farthest

If something is **far** away, it is a long way away.
दूर
*His house was **far** away.*

farm noun
farms

A **farm** is a piece of land with buildings on it where people grow crops and keep animals.
खेत

farmer noun
farmers

A **farmer** is a person who grows crops and keeps animals on a farm.
किसान

fast adjective
faster, fastest

Something that is **fast** can move quickly.
तेज़
*This car is very **fast**.*

fasten verb
fastens, fastening, fastened

When you **fasten** something, you close it up.
बाँधना/बंद करना
*She **fastened** the buttons on her coat.*

fat adjective
fatter, fattest

Someone who is **fat** has a big, round body.
मोटा

father noun
fathers

A **father** is a man who has a child.
पिता

fault noun
faults

If something bad is your **fault**, you made it happen.
गलती
*It's my **fault** that we were late.*

favourite adjective

Your **favourite** person or thing is the one you like best.
प्रिय
*My **favourite** food is cheese.*

fear *noun*

Fear is the way you feel when you think that something bad is going to happen to you.
भय/डर
*She shook with **fear**.*

feast *noun*
feasts

A **feast** is a large and special meal for a lot of people.
दावत/भोज

feather *noun*
feathers

Feathers are the soft, light things that cover a bird's body. They keep the bird warm and help it to fly.
पंख

February *noun*

February is the month after January and before March. It usually has 28 days, but once every four years, it has 29 days.
फरवरी

feed *verb*
feeds, feeding, fed

If you **feed** a person or an animal, you give them food.
खिलाना
*I **feed** my cat twice a day.*

feel *verb*
feels, feeling, felt

1 The way you **feel**, for example happy or sad, or cold or tired, is how you are at the time.
अनुभव करना
*I **feel** very upset.*

2 If you **feel** something, you touch it with your hand to see what it is like.
छूकर देखना
Feel how soft these feathers are.

feet
➡ Look at **foot**.
*Don't put your **feet** on the chair.*

fell
➡ Look at **fall**.
*She **fell** and hurt her knee.*

felt
➡ Look at **feel**.
*I **felt** angry.*

female *adjective*

A **female** person or animal could become a mother.
स्त्री

fence *noun*
fences

A **fence** is a wall made of wood or metal that goes round a piece of land.
बाड़ा
*There is a **fence** round the garden.*

fetch *verb*
fetches, fetching, fetched

If you **fetch** something, you go to where it is and bring it back.
ले आना
*He **fetched** a towel from the bathroom.*

fever *noun*
fevers

If you have a **fever** when you are ill, your body is too hot.
बुखार

few
fewer, fewest

A **few** means some, but not many.
कुछ
*She gave me a **few** sweets.*

a
b
c
d
e
f
g
h
i
j
k
l
m
n
o
p
q
r
s
t
u
v
w
x
y
z

A B C D E F G H I J K L M N O P Q R S T U V W X Y Z

field noun
fields

A **field** is a piece of land where people grow crops or keep animals.
खेत

fierce adjective
fiercer, fiercest

A **fierce** animal is very angry and might attack you.
आगबबूला/क्रुद्ध
*That dog looks very **fierce**.*

fight verb
fights, fighting, fought

When people **fight**, they try to hurt each other.
लड़ाई करना
*Two boys started to **fight** in the playground.*

fill verb
fills, filling, filled

If you **fill** something, you put so much into it that you cannot get any more in.
भरना
*She **filled** her cup with tea.*

film noun
films

A **film** is a story told in moving pictures that you watch on a screen.
चलचित्र

fin noun
fins

A **fin** is one of the thin, flat parts on a fish's body that help it to swim.
मछली के शरीर का पंख जैसा भाग

find verb
finds, finding, found

If you **find** something that has been lost, you see it after you have been looking for it.
पाना
*I can't **find** my shoes.*

fine adjective
finer, finest

1 If you say that you are **fine**, you mean that you are well or happy.
अच्छा
*I feel **fine** now.*

2 Something that is **fine** is very thin.
महीन/बारीक
*She sewed the cloth with **fine** thread.*

3 When the weather is **fine**, it is dry and sunny.
सुहावना
*It is a **fine** day.*

finger noun
fingers

Your **fingers** are the long thin parts at the end of each hand.
अँगुली
*She put the ring on her **finger**.*

finish verb
finishes, finishing, finished

When you **finish** something, you come to the end of it.
समास करना
*I **finished** my homework.*

fire noun
fires

Fire is the hot, bright flames that come from something that is burning.
आग
*The **fire** destroyed the forest.*

fire engine noun
fire engines

A **fire engine** is a large truck that carries people and equipment to stop fires.
दमकल

firework noun
fireworks

Fireworks are things that make a loud bang or flashes of bright colour when they are burned.
आतिशबाजी

firm *adjective*
firmer, firmest

Something that is **firm** is hard, and is not easy to bend.

दृढ़

first *adjective*

If a person or thing is **first**, they come before all the others.

पहला

*January is the **first** month of the year.*

fish *noun*
fish, fishes

A **fish** is an animal that lives in water. **Fish** have fins to help them swim.

मछली

fit *verb*
fits, fitting, fitted

If something **fits** you, it is the right size and shape for you.

माप का/उपयुक्त

*These shoes don't **fit** me.*

five *noun*

Five is the number **5**.

पाँच

fix *verb*
fixes, fixing, fixed

1 If you **fix** something that is broken, you mend it.
   ठीक करना

   *He **fixed** the radio.*

2 If you **fix** something to another thing, you join them together.
   लगाना

   *She **fixed** the shelf to the wall.*

flag *noun*
flags

A **flag** is a piece of cloth with a pattern on it. Each country of the world has its own **flag**.

झंडा

flame *noun*
flames

A **flame** is the hot, bright light that comes from a fire.

ज्वाला

*The **flames** almost burned her fingers.*

flash *noun*
flashes

A **flash** is a sudden bright light.

कौंध/चमक

*There was a **flash** of lightning.*

flat *adjective*
flatter, flattest

If something is **flat**, it is smooth and does not have any lumps.

सपाट

*Lay the painting on a **flat** surface until it is dry.*

flavour *noun*
flavours

The **flavour** of food is the taste that it has.

स्वाद

*They had ice cream in lots of **flavours**.*

flew

⇨ Look at **fly**.

*An aeroplane **flew** across the sky.*

flies

⇨ Look at **fly**.

*A bird **flies** by moving its wings.*

float *verb*
floats, floating, floated

1 If something **floats** in a liquid, it stays on top of it.
   जल पर तैरना

   *The boat **floated** on the water.*

2 If something **floats** in the air, it moves slowly through it.
   वायु में तैरना

   *A balloon **floated** over our heads.*

a
b
c
d
e
f
g
h
i
j
k
l
m
n
o
p
q
r
s
t
u
v
w
x
y
z

A
B
C
D
E
F
G
H
I
J
K
L
M
N
O
P
Q
R
S
T
U
V
W
X
Y
Z

flock noun
flocks

A **flock** is the name for
a group of birds or sheep.
झुंड

flood noun
floods

If there is a **flood**, a lot of water covers land that is
usually dry.
बाढ़
*We couldn't get to school because of the **flood**.*

floor noun
floors

1 A **floor** is the part of a room that you walk on.
फ़र्श
*There were carpets on the **floor**.*

2 A **floor** of a building is all the rooms in it that are
at the same height.
मंज़िल/माला
*Our house is on the first **floor**.*

flour noun

Flour is a powder made
from wheat that is used
to make bread and cakes.
आटा

flow verb
flows, flowing, flowed

If something **flows**, it moves along in a steady way
and does not stop.
बहना
*The river **flowed** through the forest.*

flower noun
flowers

A **flower** is the part of a plant
that makes seeds. **Flowers** often
have bright colours and a nice smell.
फूल

flown

⇨ Look at **fly**.
*The birds have all **flown** away.*

flu noun

If you have **flu**, you feel as if you have a very bad cold,
and your body aches.
फ़्लू

fly verb
**flies, flying,
flew, flown**

When a bird or
aeroplane **flies**, it
moves through the air.
उड़ना

fly noun
flies

A **fly** is a small insect with two thin, clear wings.
मक्खी

fog noun

Fog is a thick cloud that
is close to the ground. It is
hard to see through it.
कोहरा

fold verb
folds, folding, folded

If you **fold** something, you bend it so that one part of it
goes over another.
तह करना/मोड़ना
*He **folded** the letter and put it in the envelope.*

follow verb
follows, following, followed

If you **follow** someone, you
go along behind them.
अनुसरण करना
*We **followed** him up
the stairs.*

50

food noun
foods

Food is what people and animals eat.
भोजन

foot noun
feet

Your **feet** are the parts of your body that are at the ends of your legs, and that you stand on.
पैर

*Stand with one **foot** in front of the other.*

football noun
footballs

1 **Football** is a game played by two teams of eleven people who kick a ball and try to score goals by getting the ball into a net.
फुटबॉल का खेल

2 A **football** is the ball that you use to play football.
फुटबॉल

forehead noun
foreheads

Your **forehead** is the part of your face that is between your hair and your eyes.
माथा

*She had a bruise on her **forehead**.*

forest noun
forests

A **forest** is a place where a lot of trees grow close together.
जंगल/वन

forever

If something goes on **forever**, it never comes to an end.
हमेशा

*The film seemed to go on **forever**.*

forgave

⇨ Look at **forgive**.

*She **forgave** her brother for spoiling her drawing.*

forget verb
forgets, forgetting, forgot, forgotten

If you **forget** something, you do not remember it.
भूलना

*Don't **forget** to lock the door.*

forgive verb
forgives, forgiving, forgave, forgiven

If you **forgive** someone who has done something bad, you stop being angry with them.
माफ़ करना

*Please **forgive** me for being late.*

forgot

⇨ Look at **forget**.

*She **forgot** to bring any money.*

forgotten

⇨ Look at **forget**.

*I have **forgotten** my keys.*

fork noun
forks

A **fork** is a tool with three or four thin, sharp points that you use to eat food with.
काँटा

fortnight noun
fortnights

A **fortnight** is two weeks.
पखवाड़ा

forwards

If you move **forwards**, you move towards the front.
आगे

*They ran backwards and **forwards** trying to catch the ball.*

a
b
c
d
e
f
g
h
i
j
k
l
m
n
o
p
q
r
s
t
u
v
w
x
y
z

51

A
B
C
D
E
F
G
H
I
J
K
L
M
N
O
P
Q
R
S
T
U
V
W
X
Y
Z

fought

⇨ Look at **fight**.

*The knights **fought** with swords.*

found

⇨ Look at **find**.

*She **found** her lost dog.*

four *noun*

Four is the number .

चार

fox *noun*
foxes

A **fox** is an animal that looks like a dog with red fur and a long, thick tail.

लोमड़ी

fraction *noun*
fractions

A **fraction** is a part of a whole number.

भिन्न

*A half and a quarter are both **fractions**.*

frame *noun*
frames

A **frame** is a piece of wood, metal or plastic that fits around the edge of a picture, a window, or a door.

चौखटा

frame

freckles *noun*

Freckles are light brown spots that some people have on their skin.

चित्ती

*His face was covered with **freckles**.*

free *adjective*
freer, freest

1 If something is **free**, you can have it without paying any money for it.

मुफ़्त

*If you buy a cup of coffee, you get a **free** cake.*

2 If you are **free**, you can do what you like or go where you like.

आज़ाद

*You are **free** to come here any time.*

freeze *verb*
freezes, freezing, froze, frozen

1 When water **freezes**, it is so cold that it becomes ice.

जमना

2 If you **freeze** food, you make it very cold so that it will not go bad.

जमाना

fresh *adjective*
fresher, freshest

1 If food is **fresh**, it has been picked or made a short time ago.

ताज़ा

*Eat some **fresh** fruit every day.*

2 **Fresh** water has no salt in it. The water in rivers is **fresh**.

मीठा/ताज़ा

3 **Fresh** air is clean and cool.

ताज़ा

Friday *noun*
Fridays

Friday is the day after Thursday and before Saturday.

शुक्रवार

*He went home on **Friday**.*

fridge *noun*
fridges

A **fridge** is a cupboard that uses electricity to keep food cold and fresh.

फ़्रिज

*Put the butter in the **fridge**.*

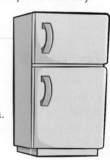

fried

⇨ Look at **fry**.
*She **fried** some eggs.*

friend *noun*
friends

A **friend** is someone you know and like, and who likes you too.
मित्र/दोस्त

friendly *adjective*
friendlier, friendliest

If someone is **friendly**, they like to meet other people, and are nice to them.
मित्र भाव से

frighten *verb*
frightens, frightening, frightened

If something **frightens** you, it makes you feel afraid.
डराना
*Loud noises **frighten** her.*

frog *noun*
frogs

A **frog** is a small animal with smooth skin, big eyes, and long back legs that it uses for jumping. **Frogs** live near water.
मेंढक

front *noun*
fronts

The **front** of something is the part that comes first or the part that you usually see first.
सामने का भाग
*She stood at the **front** of the queue.*

frost *noun*

Frost is ice that looks like white powder. It covers things outside when the weather is very cold.
पाला/तुषार

frown *verb*
frowns, frowning, frowned

When you **frown**, lines appear on your forehead because you are cross or because you are thinking about something.
त्योरी चढ़ाना

froze

⇨ Look at **freeze**.
*It was so cold that the lake **froze**.*

frozen

⇨ Look at **freeze**.
*The water had **frozen** into ice.*

fruit *noun*
fruits

Fruit is the part of a plant or a tree that has the seeds in it. You can eat many **fruits**, for example apples, bananas, and strawberries.
फल

fry *verb*
fries, frying, fried

When you **fry** food, you cook it in hot oil or butter.
तलना
***Fry** the onions until they are brown.*

full *adjective*
fuller, fullest

If something is **full**, it has so much in it that it cannot hold any more.
भरा
*The bottle is **full**.*

a
b
c
d
e
f
g
h
i
j
k
l
m
n
o
p
q
r
s
t
u
v
w
x
y
z

fun *noun*

When you have **fun**, you enjoy doing something and you feel happy.

मज़ा

*They had **fun** at the beach.*

funny *adjective*
funnier, funniest

1 If something is **funny**, it makes you laugh.

मज़ाकिया/हास्यप्रद

*He told me a **funny** joke.*

2 **Funny** also means strange.

अजीब

*The car is making a **funny** noise.*

fur *noun*

Fur is the soft hair that covers the bodies of many animals.

रोआँ

*Pandas have black and white **fur**.*

furniture *noun*

Furniture is the name for all the big things, for example tables, chairs, or beds, that people have in their houses.

फ़र्नीचर

*We bought new **furniture** for the bedroom.*

future *noun*

The **future** is the time that will come after the present time.

आगामी/भविष्य

*In the **future**, people will travel to other planets.*

Gg

gale *noun*
gales

A **gale** is a very strong wind.

आँधी

game *noun*
games

1 A **game** is something you play that has rules, for example football.

खेल

2 Children also play a **game** when they pretend to be other people.

खेल

*We played a **game** of pirates.*

gap *noun*
gaps

A **gap** is a space between two things.

अंतराल/अंतर

*There was a **gap** between the curtains.*

garage *noun*
garages

1 A **garage** is a building where you keep a car.

गैराज - गाड़ी रखने की जगह

2 A **garage** is also a place where you can get your car repaired.

गैराज - गाड़ी की मरम्मत करने की जगह

garden *noun*
gardens

A **garden** is a piece of land near a house where people can grow grass, flowers, and vegetables.

बगीचा

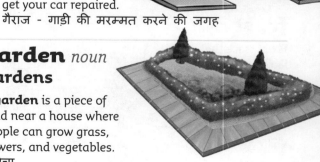

gas *noun*
gases

A **gas** is anything, for example air, that is not solid or a liquid.
गैस

gate *noun*
gates

A **gate** is a kind of door in a wall, a fence, or a hedge.
फाटक

gave

⇨ Look at **give**.
*She **gave** me a present.*

gentle *adjective*
gentler, gentlest

If you are **gentle**, you are careful and not rough.
सौम्य
*Be **gentle** when you hold the baby.*

get *verb*
gets, getting, got

1   You can use **get** to mean the same as "become".
होना
*We should go before it **gets** dark.*

2   If you **get** somewhere, you arrive there.
पहुँचना
*He **got** home at noon.*

3   If you **get** something, someone gives it to you.
पाना
*I **got** a bike for my birthday.*

4   If you **get** something, you go to where it is and bring it back.
लाना
*He went to **get** a cup of coffee.*

ghost *noun*
ghosts

A **ghost** is a dead person who some people think they can see and hear.
भूत/प्रेतात्मा

giant *adjective*

Something that is **giant** is very large.
विशालकाय
*They watched the film on a **giant** TV screen.*

giraffe *noun*
giraffes

A **giraffe** is a very tall animal with a long neck, long legs, and dark spots on its body.
जिराफ़

girl *noun*
girls

A **girl** is a child or a young person who is a female.
लड़की

give *verb*
gives, giving, gave, given

If you **give** someone something, you let them have it to keep.
देना
*We always **give** our mother flowers on her birthday.*

glad *adjective*
gladder, gladdest

If you are **glad**, you are happy about something.
ख़ुश
*I'm **glad** you can come to my party.*

glass *noun*
glasses

1   **Glass** is a hard, clear material that is used to make things like windows and bottles. It is quite easy to break **glass**.
काँच
*The salad was in a **glass** bowl.*

2   A **glass** is also a container made from glass that you can drink out of.
गिलास
*He filled his **glass** with milk.*

glasses *noun*

Glasses are two pieces of plastic or glass in a frame that people wear in front of their eyes to help them to see better.
चश्मा

a
b
c
d
e
f
g
h
i
j
k
l
m
n
o
p
q
r
s
t
u
v
w
x
y
z

A
B
C
D
E
F
G
H
I
J
K
L
M
N
O
P
Q
R
S
T
U
V
W
X
Y
Z

glove *noun*
gloves

Gloves are things that you wear over your hands to keep them warm. **Gloves** have one part for your thumb and one for all your fingers.
दस्ताना

glue *noun*

You use **glue** to stick things together.
गोंद

go *verb*
goes, going, went, gone

1 If you **go** somewhere, you move there from another place.
जाना
Can we go to the park?

2 If you say that something is **going** to happen, you mean that it will happen.
होना
He's going to leave soon.

goal *noun*
goals

In games like football, the **goal** is the place that you try to get the ball in to, to score a point.
गोल–वह स्थान जिसमें खिलाड़ी गेंद को डालने की कोशिश करते हैं

goat *noun*
goats

A **goat** is an animal about the size of a sheep. **Goats** have horns, and hair on their chin that looks like a beard.
बकरी

gold *noun*

Gold is a valuable, yellow metal that is used to make things like rings and necklaces, and also coins.
स्वर्ण/सोना

goldfish *noun*
goldfish

A **goldfish** is a small orange fish that people often keep as a pet.
गोल्डफ़िश-एक प्रकार की छोटी सुनहरी मछली

gone

⇨ Look at **go**.
She has gone home.

good *adjective*
better, best

1 If you say that something is **good**, you like it.
अच्छा
That was a good film.

2 If you are **good**, you behave well.
अच्छा
Be good while I am out.

3 If you are **good** at something, you do it well.
अच्छा
She is good at drawing.

goodbye

You say **goodbye** to someone when one of you is going away.
अलविदा

good night

You say **good night** to someone late in the evening before you go home or go to bed.
शुभरात्रि

goose *noun*
geese

A **goose** is a large bird with a long neck that lives near water.
कलहंस–बत्तख जैसा पक्षी

gorilla *noun*
gorillas

A **gorilla** is a large, strong animal with long arms, black fur, and a black face.
वनमानुष

got

⇨ Look at **get**.
They soon got tired of the game.

grain *noun*
grains

1 A **grain** is the seed of a cereal plant, for example rice or wheat.
अनाज

2 A **grain** of something, for example sand or salt, is a tiny piece of it.
कण

gram *noun*
grams

A **gram** is used for measuring how heavy things are.
ग्राम

*There are about 400 **grams** of jam in this jar.*

grandfather *noun*
grandfathers

Your **grandfather** is your father's father or your mother's father.
दादा/नाना

grandmother *noun*
grandmothers

Your **grandmother** is your father's mother or your mother's mother.
दादी/नानी

grape *noun*
grapes

A **grape** is a small, round, green or purple fruit that grows in bunches.
अंगूर

grapefruit *noun*
grapefruits

A **grapefruit** is a large, round, yellow fruit with a sour taste.
चकोतरा

graph *noun*
graphs

In maths, a **graph** is a picture that uses lines or shapes to show numbers.
लेखा-चित्र

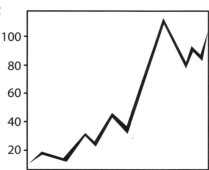

grass *noun*
grasses

Grass is a green plant with very thin leaves that cover the ground in fields and gardens.
घास

great *adjective*
greater, greatest

1 **Great** means very large.
विशाल
*The king lived in a **great** palace.*

2 **Great** also means very important.
महान/महत्
*The computer was a **great** invention.*

3 If you say that something is **great**, you mean that it is very good.
बढ़िया/शानदार
*We had a **great** time.*

greedy *adjective*
greedier, greediest

If someone is **greedy**, they want to have more of something than they need.
लालची

*He was so **greedy** that he ate the whole cake.*

green *noun*

Green is the colour of grass or leaves.
हरा
*Her dress is **green**.*

grew

⇨ Look at **grow**.
*The tree **grew** to a great height.*

grey *noun*

Grey is a mixture of black and white, like the colour of clouds when rain is falling.
स्लेटी

ground *noun*

The **ground** is the earth or other surface that you walk on outside.
ज़मीन/भूमि

a b c d e f **g** h i j k l m n o p q r s t u v w x y z

57

group *noun*
groups

A **group** is a number of people or things that are together, or that belong together.
समूह

grow *verb*
grows, growing, grew, grown

When something **grows**, it gets bigger.
विकसित होना/बढ़ना
*The puppy **grew** into a huge dog.*

guess *verb*
guesses, guessing, guessed

If you **guess**, you say what you think is true about something, but you do not really know if you are right.
अनुमान लगाना
*Can you **guess** how old he is?*

guinea pig *noun*
guinea pigs

A **guinea pig** is a small animal with fur and no tail that people often keep as a pet.
गिनी पिग - एक छोटा जानवर

guitar *noun*
guitars

A **guitar** is an instrument with strings that you play by pressing the strings with one hand and pulling them with the other hand.
गिटार

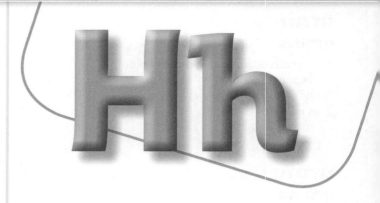

had
⇨ Look at **have**.
*We **had** a nice time.*

hadn't
Hadn't is short for **had not**.
नहीं किया
*I **hadn't** seen them for a long time.*

hair *noun*
Hair is the soft, fine threads that grow on your head and on the bodies of many animals.
बाल
*I wash my **hair** every night.*

half *noun*
halves

A **half** is one of two equal parts that make up a whole thing.
आधा
*We each had **half** of the cake.*

halves
⇨ Look at **half**.
*Cut the apples into **halves**.*

hamster *noun*
hamsters

A **hamster** is a small animal that looks like a fat mouse with a short tail. People often keep **hamsters** as pets.
चूहे जैसा एक पशु

hand *noun*
hands

Your **hands** are the parts of your body that are at the ends of your arms, and that you use to hold things. A **hand** has four fingers and a thumb.
हाथ
*I put my **hand** in my pocket and took out the letter.*

handle *noun*
handles

1 A **handle** is something that is joined to a door, a window, or a drawer, that you use to open and close it.
हत्था/मूठ
*She pulled the **handle** of the drawer.*

2 A **handle** is also the part of something, for example a tool or a bag, that you use to hold it.
हत्था/मूठ
*Hold the knife by its **handle**.*

hang *verb*
hangs, hanging, hung

If you **hang** something somewhere, you fix the top of it to something so that it does not touch the ground.
लटकाना
*She **hung** her coat on a peg.*

happen *verb*
happens, happening, happened

When something **happens**, it takes place.
घटित होना
*What's **happening** in the playground?*

happy *adjective*
happier, happiest

When you are **happy**, you feel pleased about something.
खुश

hard *adjective*
harder, hardest

1 Something that is **hard** is solid, and it is not easy to bend it or break it.
कड़ा/सख्त या कठोर
*The glass broke on the **hard** floor.*

2 If something is **hard**, you have to try a lot to do it or to understand it.
कठिन
*These sums are quite **hard**.*

has

⇨ Look at **have**.
*He **has** a sister.*

hasn't

Hasn't is short for **has not**.
नहीं है
*She **hasn't** anything to do.*

hat *noun*
hats

A **hat** is something that you can wear on your head.
टोप

hatch *verb*
hatches, hatching, hatched

When a baby bird or other animal **hatches**, it comes out of its egg by breaking the shell. You can also say that the egg **hatches**.
अंडे से बच्चा निकलना

hate *verb*
hates, hating, hated

If you **hate** a person or a thing, you feel that you do not like them at all.
घृणा करना
*I **hate** onions.*

have *verb*
has, having, had

1 If you **have** something, it belongs to you.
होना/रखना
*Do you **have** any pets?*

2 When you **have** something, you feel it, or it happens to you.
ग्रस्त होना/होना
*I **have** a bad cold.*

A
B
C
D
E
F
G
H
I
J
K
L
M
N
O
P
Q
R
S
T
U
V
W
X
Y
Z

haven't

Haven't is short for **have not**.
नहीं है
I **haven't** any chocolate left.

hay *noun*

Hay is dry grass that is used to feed animals.
भूसा

head *noun*
heads

1 Your **head** is the part of your body at the top that has your eyes, ears, nose, mouth, and brain in it.
सिर
*The ball hit him on the **head**.*

2 The **head** of something is the person who is its leader.
मुखिया
*He is the **head** of the school.*

heal *verb*
heals, healing, healed

If something like a broken bone **heals**, it gets better.
घाव भरना

healthy *adjective*
healthier, healthiest

1 Someone who is **healthy** is well and strong and is not often ill.
स्वस्थ
*People need exercise to stay **healthy**.*

2 Something that is **healthy** is good for you.
स्वास्थ्यवर्धक
*Eat **healthy** food like fruit and vegetables.*

hear *verb*
hears, hearing, heard

When you **hear** a sound, you notice it through your ears.
सुनना
*I **heard** a dog barking.*

heart *noun*
hearts

Your **heart** is the part inside you that makes the blood move around your body.
हृदय
*His **heart** was going fast.*

heavy *adjective*
heavier, heaviest

Something that is **heavy** weighs a lot.
भारी
*This bag is very **heavy**.*

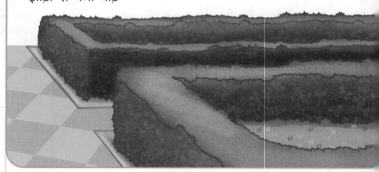

he'd

1 **He'd** is short for **he had**.
वह कर चुका है
He'd seen it before.

2 **He'd** is also short for **he would**.
वह करेगा
He'd like them.

hedge *noun*
hedges

A **hedge** is a row of bushes growing close together that makes a kind of wall. You often see **hedges** around fields.
झाड़ी से बनी बाड़

heel *noun*
heels

Your **heels** are the parts of your feet at the back, below your ankles.
एड़ी
*He dragged his **heels** along the ground.*

height *noun*
heights

Your **height** is how tall you are.
कद/ऊँचाई
*We all measured our **heights**.*

held

⇨ Look at **hold**.

*Mum **held** my hand as we crossed the road.*

helicopter *noun*
helicopters

A **helicopter** is a small aircraft with long blades on top that go round very quickly. **Helicopters** can fly straight up and down and stay in one place in the air.

हेलीकॉप्टर

he'll

He'll is short for **he will**.

वह करेगा

He'll come back soon.

hello

You say **hello** to someone when you meet them.

नमस्कार

help *verb*
helps, helping, helped

If you **help** someone, you make it easier for them to do something.

सहायता करना

*He **helped** me with my homework.*

hen *noun*
hens

A **hen** is a chicken that is a female. People often eat **hens'** eggs as food.

मुर्गी

her

You use **her** to talk about a woman or a girl, or to say that something belongs to a woman or a girl.

उसका (लड़की/स्त्री के लिए)

*I gave **her** back **her** pen.*

herd *noun*
herds

A **herd** is a large group of animals that lives together.

झुंड

*We saw a **herd** of deer in the forest.*

here

Here means the place where you are.

यहाँ

*Come and sit **here**.*

hers

You use **hers** to say that something belongs to a woman or a girl.

उसका (स्त्री)

*She said that the bag was **hers**.*

herself

You use **herself** when you want to say that something a woman or a girl does has an effect on her.

स्वयं (स्त्री)

*She pulled **herself** out of the water.*

he's

He's is short for **he is**.

वह है

He's six years old.

hexagon *noun*
hexagons

A **hexagon** is a shape with six straight sides.

षट्भुज

hid

⇨ Look at **hide**.

*They **hid** in the cupboard.*

A
B
C
D
E
F
G
H
I
J
K
L
M
N
O
P
Q
R
S
T
U
V
W
X
Y
Z

hidden

⇨ Look at **hide**.

*He was **hidden** under the bed.*

hide *verb*
hides, hiding, hid, hidden

1 If you **hide** something, you put it where no one can see it or find it.
छुपाना
*He **hid** his bike behind the wall.*

2 If you **hide** what you feel, you do not let people know about it.
छुपाना
*She tried to **hide** how angry she was.*

high *adjective*
higher, highest

1 Something that is **high** is tall or is a long way above the ground.
ऊँचा
*There was a **high** wall around the house.*

2 **High** also means great in amount or strength.
अधिक
*They charged us a **high** price.*

3 A **high** sound or voice goes up a long way.
ऊँचा
*She spoke in a **high** voice.*

hill *noun*
hills

A **hill** is a piece of land that is higher than the land around it. **Hills** are not as high as mountains.
पहाड़ी

him

You use **him** to talk about a man or a boy.
उसे (पुरुष)
*We met **him** at the station.*

himself

You use **himself** when you want to say that something a man or a boy does has an effect on him.
खुद (पुरुष)
*He fell and hurt **himself**.*

hippopotamus *noun*
hippopotamuses or hippopotami

A **hippopotamus** is a large animal with short legs and thick skin that lives near rivers.
दरियाई घोड़ा

his

You use **his** to say that something belongs to a man or a boy.
उसका (लड़के/पुरुष के लिए)
*He showed me **his** new football.*

history *noun*

History is the story of what has happened in the past.
इतिहास

hit *verb*
hits, hitting, hit

If you **hit** something, you touch it with a lot of strength.
मारना
*She **hit** the ball with the bat.*

hive *noun*
hives

A **hive** is a place where bees live.
छत्ता

hold *verb*
holds, holding, held

1   When you **hold** something, you have it in your hands or your arms.
पकड़ना
*She **held** the baby in her arms.*

2   If something **holds** an amount of something, then that is how much it has room for inside.
संभाले रखना/जगह होना
*The theatre **holds** 400 people.*

hole *noun*
holes

A **hole** is a gap or a hollow place in something.
छेद
*We dug a **hole** in the ground.*

holiday *noun*
holidays

A **holiday** is a time when you do not need to work or go to school.
छुट्टी

hollow *adjective*

Something that is **hollow** has an empty space inside it.
खोखला
*The owl's nest was in a **hollow** tree.*

home *noun*
homes

Your **home** is the place where you live.
घर
*We stayed at **home** and watched TV.*

homework *noun*

Homework is something like sums that a teacher gives you to work on at home.
गृहकार्य

honest *adjective*

If someone is **honest**, they do not tell lies, and you can believe what they say.
ईमानदार

honey *noun*

Honey is a sweet, very thick liquid that is made by bees. You can eat **honey** on bread.
शहद

hoof *noun*
hooves

A **hoof** is the hard part of a horse's foot. Deer and cows also have **hooves**.
खुर

hop *verb*
hops, hopping, hopped

1   If you **hop**, you jump on one foot.
एक पैर से कूदना

2   When animals or birds **hop**, they jump with two feet together.
फुदकना

hope *verb*
hopes, hoping, hoped

If you **hope** that something will happen, you want it to happen.
आशा करना
*I **hope** you feel better soon.*

horn *noun*
horns

1   A **horn** is one of the hard bones with sharp points that grow out of some animals' heads. Goats and bulls have **horns**.
सींग

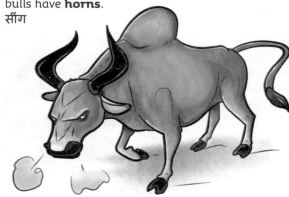

2   A **horn** is also an instrument that you blow into to make music.
शृंगी - एक वाद्ययंत्र

horrible *adjective*

If something is **horrible**, it is very nasty.
भयानक
*There was a **horrible** smell.*

A
B
C
D
E
F
G
H
I
J
K
L
M
N
O
P
Q
R
S
T
U
V
W
X
Y
Z

horse *noun*
horses

A **horse** is a large animal with a long tail and four legs. People ride on **horses** or use them to pull things along.
घोड़ा

hospital *noun*
hospitals

A **hospital** is a building where doctors and nurses care for people who are ill or hurt.
अस्पताल

hot *adjective*
hotter, hottest

If something is **hot**, it is very warm.
गर्म

*Don't touch the plate – it's **hot**.*

hour *noun*
hours

An **hour** is used for measuring time. There are sixty minutes in an **hour**, and twenty-four **hours** in a day.
घंटा

house *noun*
houses

A **house** is a building where people live.
मकान

*Come to my **house** for dinner.*

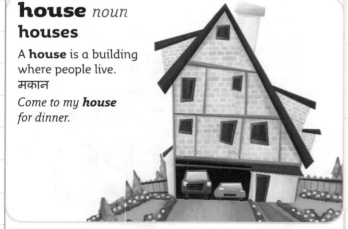

how

1   You use the word **how** when you ask about the way that something happens or the way that you do something.
कैसे

   ***How** do you spell your name?*

2   You also use **how** when you ask about an amount.
कितना

   ***How** many people were at the party?*

hug *verb*
hugs, hugging, hugged

When you **hug** someone, you put your arms around them and hold them close to you.
आलिंगन करना

*She **hugged** me as we said goodbye.*

huge *adjective*

Something that is **huge** is very big.
विशाल

*Elephants are **huge** animals.*

human *adjective*

Something that is **human** is to do with people, and not animals or machines.
मानवीय

*There are over 200 bones in the **human** body.*

hundred *noun*

A **hundred** is the number 100.
सौ

hung
⇨ Look at **hang**.
*He **hung** from the bars.*

hungry *adjective*
hungrier, hungriest

If you are **hungry**, you want to eat something.
भूखा

hunt *verb*
hunts, hunting, hunted

1   When animals **hunt**, they chase another animal to kill it for food.
शिकार करना
*The lions **hunted** a zebra.*

2   If you **hunt** for something, you try to find it.
तलाश करना / खोजना
*I **hunted** for my keys.*

hurry *verb*
hurries, hurrying, hurried

If you **hurry**, you move quickly or do something quickly.
जल्दी करना
*We'll be late if we don't **hurry**.*

hurt *verb*
hurts, hurting, hurt

If you **hurt** someone or something, you make them feel pain.
चोट पहुँचाना
*I fell over and **hurt** my leg yesterday.*

husband *noun*
husbands

A woman's **husband** is the man she is married to.
पति

hut *noun*
huts

A **hut** is a small building with one or two rooms. **Huts** are made of wood, mud, or grass.
झोपड़ी

hutch *noun*
hutches

A **hutch** is a kind of cage made of wood and wire, where people keep rabbits and other small pets.
पिंजरा

I

You use **I** to talk about yourself.
मैं
I like chocolate.

ice *noun*

Ice is water that has frozen. It is very cold and hard.
बर्फ़
*The ground was covered with **ice**.*

ice cream *noun*

Ice cream is a very cold, sweet food that is made from frozen milk or cream.
आइसक्रीम

icicle *noun*
icicles

An **icicle** is a long piece of ice with a point at the end that hangs down from something. **Icicles** are made from dripping water that has frozen.
हिमलंब / बर्फ़ की लटकती चट्टान

I'd

1   **I'd** is short for **I had**.
मैं कर चुका हूँ
I'd been there before.

2   **I'd** is also short for **I would**.
मैं करूँगा
I'd like to go to the zoo.

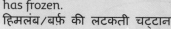

idea *noun*
ideas

An **idea** is something new that you have thought of.
विचार
*He had an **idea** for a story.*

ill *adjective*

When you are **ill**,
you do not feel well.
बीमार
*She is too **ill** to go to school.*

I'll

I'll is short for **I will**.
मैं करूँगा
I'll come back tomorrow.

illness *noun*
illnesses

If you have an **illness**, you do not feel well.
बीमारी
*He has just had a very bad **illness**.*

I'm

I'm is short for **I am**.
मैं हूँ
I'm hungry.

imagine *verb*
imagines, imagining, imagined

If you **imagine** something, you make a picture of it in your mind.
कल्पना करना
Imagine that you are a cat.

immediately

If you do something **immediately**, you do it now.
तत्काल
*Stop that noise **immediately**!*

important *adjective*

1   If something is **important**, people care about it and think about it a lot.
महत्वपूर्ण
*It is **important** not to tell lies.*

2   If someone is **important**, people pay a lot of attention to what they say and do.
महत्वपूर्ण
*She is a very **important** person.*

impossible *adjective*

If something is **impossible**, it cannot be done, or it cannot happen.
असंभव
*It is **impossible** to see in the dark.*

in

1   **In** means not outside.
में/ के अंदर
*The juice is **in** the fridge.*

2   You also use **in** to say when something happens.
में
*He was born **in** March.*

inch *noun*
inches

An **inch** is used for measuring the length of something. There are about two and half centimetres in an **inch**.
इंच

indoors

If you are **indoors**, you are inside a building.
घर के भीतर

information *noun*

Information about something is facts that tell you about it.
सूचना
*I need some **information** about birds.*

ink *noun*

Ink is a liquid that you use to write or print with. Pens have **ink** inside them.
स्याही

insect *noun*
insects

An **insect** is a small animal with six legs, for example a bee or a beetle.
Many **insects** have wings and can fly.
कीड़ा

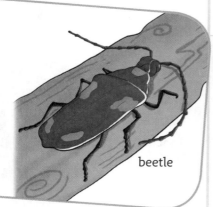

beetle

inside

1 If something is **inside** another thing, it is in it.
अंदर
*There was a letter **inside** the envelope.*

2 **Inside** also means indoors.
भीतर
*He went **inside** and locked the door.*

instructions *noun*

Instructions are words or pictures that tell you how to do something.
निर्देश
*Here are the **instructions** for building the tent.*

instrument *noun*
instruments

1 An **instrument** is a tool that you use to do something.
उपकरण
*The doctor used an **instrument** to look in my ears.*

2 An **instrument** is also something, for example a piano or a guitar, that you use to make music.
वाद्ययंत्र
*He plays three **instruments**.*

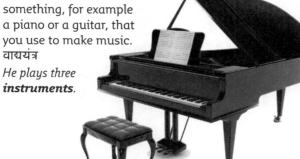

intelligent *adjective*

If a person is **intelligent**, they are able to understand and learn things quickly.
बुद्धिमान

interesting *adjective*

If something is **interesting**, you want to know more about it.
रोचक

Internet *noun*

The **Internet** is something that joins a computer to other computers all over the world. You send emails using the **Internet**.
इंटरनेट

interrupt *verb*
interrupts, interrupting, interrupted

If you **interrupt** someone, you say or do something that makes them stop in the middle of what they are doing.
टोकना
*Don't **interrupt** the teacher when she's talking.*

invention *noun*
inventions

An **invention** is something that someone has made, and that nobody has ever thought of or made before.
आविष्कार
*His new **invention** is a car that can fly.*

invisible *adjective*

If something is **invisible**, you cannot see it.
अदृश्य

invite *verb*
invites, inviting, invited

If you **invite** someone to something, for example a party, you ask them to come to it.
आमंत्रित करना

a
b
c
d
e
f
g
h
i
j
k
l
m
n
o
p
q
r
s
t
u
v
w
x
y
z

A
B
C
D
E
F
G
H
I
J
K
L
M
N
O
P
Q
R
S
T
U
V
W
X
Y
Z

iron noun
irons

1 **Iron** is a strong, hard, grey metal.
लोहा

2 An **iron** is a piece of equipment with a flat bottom that gets hot. You move the bottom over clothes to make them smooth.
इस्तरी

is
➡ Look at **be**.
She is six years old.

island noun
islands

An **island** is a piece of land that has water all around it.
द्वीप

isn't
Isn't is short for **is not**.
नहीं है
He isn't very happy.

it
You use **it** to talk about a thing or an animal.
यह/वह
This is a good book – have you read it?

its
You use **its** to say that something belongs to a thing or an animal.
इसका/उसका
The lion lifted its head.

it's
It's is short for **it is**.
यह है
It's one o'clock.

I've
I've is short for **I have**.
मैं कर चुका हूँ
I've been playing football.

jacket noun
jackets

A **jacket** is a short coat.
जैकेट

jam noun

Jam is a soft, sweet food that is made from fruit and sugar.
जैम
I love strawberry jam on my bread.

January noun

January is the month after December and before February. It has 31 days.
जनवरी

jar noun
jars

A **jar** is a glass container with a lid that is used for storing food.
मर्तबान
Make sure you put the lid back on the jar.

jaw noun
jaws

Your **jaws** are the top and bottom bones of your mouth.
जबड़ा

jaw

jeans *noun*

Jeans are blue trousers with pockets at the front and back.
जीन्स
*Everyone on the trip wore **jeans** and a bright T-shirt.*

jelly *noun*

Jelly is a clear, sweet food that is solid but soft.
जेली
*We had birthday cake, then **jelly** and ice cream.*

jet *noun*
jets

A **jet** is a plane that flies very fast.
जेट जहाज

jewel *noun*
jewels

1 A **jewel** is a valuable stone, like a diamond.
रत्न

2 **Jewels** are things made with valuable stones, that you wear to decorate your body.
आभूषण/गहना
*She put the **jewels** in the box and turned the key.*

jigsaw *noun*
jigsaws

A **jigsaw** is a picture on cardboard that has been cut up into pieces. You have to fit them together again.
जिग्सॉ पहेली
*The children put the last pieces in the **jigsaw**.*

job *noun*
jobs

A **job** is the work that a person does to earn money.
नौकरी
*My sister wants to get a **job**.*

join *verb*
joins, joining, joined

1 If you **join** a group of people, you become one of the group.
शामिल होना
*Come and **join** the music group after school on Mondays.*

2 When things **join**, or you **join** them, they come together.
जोड़ना
*They **joined** hands and danced.*

joke *noun*
jokes

A **joke** is something that someone says to make you laugh.
चुटकुला
*Grandfather always tells us **jokes** after dinner.*

journey *noun*
journeys

When you make a **journey**, you travel from one place to another.
यात्रा
*It was a difficult **journey** that took several days.*

jug *noun*
jugs

A **jug** is a container with a handle. You use a **jug** for pouring liquids.
जग
*There is a **jug** of cold water on the table.*

juice *noun*
juices

Juice is the liquid from a fruit or vegetable.
रस
*He had a large glass of fresh orange **juice**.*

a
b
c
d
e
f
g
h
i
j
k
l
m
n
o
p
q
r
s
t
u
v
w
x
y
z

A
B
C
D
E
F
G
H
I
J
K
L
M
N
O
P
Q
R
S
T
U
V
W
X
Y
Z

July noun

July is the month after June and before August. It has 31 days.
जुलाई

jump verb
jumps, jumping, jumped

When you **jump**, you bend your knees and push yourself into the air.
कूदना
*I **jumped** over the fence.*

jumper noun
jumpers

You wear a **jumper** to keep yourself warm. It has sleeves and covers the top half of your body.
कुरती

June noun

June is the month after May and before July. It has 30 days.
जून

jungle noun
jungles

A **jungle** is a thick, wet forest in a hot country.
जंगल
*They followed the path deep into the **jungle**.*

just

If you **just** did something, you did it a very short time ago.
अभी-अभी
*We **just** got home after an awful journey.*

kangaroo noun
kangaroos

A **kangaroo** is a large Australian animal that carries its babies in a pocket on its stomach.
कंगारू

keen adjective
keener, keenest

If you are **keen**, you want to do something very much.
उत्सुक
*Everyone was **keen** to help.*

keep verb
keeps, keeping, kept

1 If someone **keeps** away from a place, they do not go near it.
रहना
***Keep** away from the road.*

2 If someone **keeps** still or warm, they stay like that.
बनाए रखना
*We lit a fire to **keep** warm.*
*"**Keep** still!"*

3 If you **keep** doing something, you do it many times or you do it some more.
जारी रखना/करते रहना
*I **keep** forgetting to take my umbrella.*

4 When you **keep** something, you store it somewhere.
रखना
*She **kept** her money under the bed.*

kennel noun
kennels

A **kennel** is a small house where a dog can sleep.
कुत्ता घर

kept

⇨ Look at **keep**.
*She **kept** her head down.*

kettle *noun*
kettles

A **kettle** is a metal container with a lid and a handle, that you use for boiling water.
केतली

*Mum put the **kettle** on and made some tea.*

key *noun*
keys

1 A **key** is a piece of metal that opens or closes a lock.
चाबी
*They put the **key** in the door and it opened.*

2 The **keys** on a computer or instrument are the buttons that you press on it.
कुंजी
*Press the "Enter" **key**.*

kick *verb*
kicks, kicking, kicked

If you **kick** something, you hit it with your foot.
पैर से मारना / ठोकर मारना
*He **kicked** the ball really hard.*

kid *noun*
kids

A **kid** is a child.
बच्चा
*They have three **kids**.*

kill *verb*
kills, killing, killed

To **kill** a living thing is to make it die.
मार डालना
*The earthquake **killed** 62 people.*

kilogram *noun*
kilograms

A **kilogram** is used for measuring how heavy things are. There are 1,000 grams in a **kilogram**.
किलोग्राम
*The box weighs 4.5 **kilograms**.*

kilometre *noun*
kilometres

A **kilometre** is used for measuring distance. There are 1,000 metres in a **kilometre**, which is about 0.62 miles.
किलोमीटर

kind *noun*
kinds

A **kind** of thing is a type or sort of that thing.
प्रकार
*What **kind** of car is that?*

kind *adjective*
kinder, kindest

Someone who is **kind** is friendly and helps you.
दयालु
*Thank you for being so **kind** to me.*

king *noun*
kings

A **king** is a man who rules a country.
राजा
*We saw the **king** and queen arriving.*

kiss *verb*
kisses, kissing, kissed

If you **kiss** someone, you touch them with your lips.
चूमना
*We **kissed** goodbye at the airport.*

kitchen *noun*
kitchens

A **kitchen** is a room that is used for cooking.
रसोईघर

a b c d e f g h i j k l m n o p q r s t u v w x y z

kite noun
kites

A **kite** is a toy that you fly in the wind at the end of a long string.
पतंग
*We went to the beach to fly **kites**.*

kitten noun
kittens

A **kitten** is a very young cat.
बिलौटा

knee noun
knees

Your **knee** is the part in the middle of your leg where it bends.
घुटना
*I fell over and hurt my **knee**.*

kneel verb
kneels, kneeling, knelt

When you **kneel**, you bend your legs and rest on one or both of your knees.
घुटने टेकना
*She **knelt** down beside the bed.*

knew
➡ Look at **know**.
*I **knew** all the kids at the party.*

knife noun
knives

A **knife** is a sharp metal tool that you use to cut things.
चाकू
*I finished and put down my **knife** and fork.*

knight noun
knights

In the past, a **knight** was a soldier who rode a horse.
घोड़े पर सवार योद्धा

knit verb
knits, knitting, knitted

If you **knit** something, you make it from a long piece of wool by using two special sticks.
बुनना
*My grandmother sat **knitting**.*

knives
➡ Look at **knife**.
*We put all the **knives** away in their box.*

knock verb
knocks, knocking, knocked

If you **knock** on something, you hit it to make a noise.
खड़काना
*She went to his house and **knocked** on the door.*

knot noun
knots

You make a **knot** when you tie two pieces of something together.
गाँठ
*He picked up the rope and tied a **knot** in it.*

know verb
knows, knowing, knew, known

1 If you **know** something, you have that information in your mind.
जानना
*You should **know** the answer to that question.*

2 If you **know** a person, you have met them and spoken to them.
जानना
*I didn't **know** any of the other people in the class.*

A
B
C
D
E
F
G
H
I
J
K
L
M
N
O
P
Q
R
S
T
U
V
W
X
Y
Z

Ll

label *noun*
labels

A **label** is a small note on something that gives you information about it.
चिप्पी/सूचक पत्र
The prices are on the labels.

lace *noun*
laces

1 **Lace** is a pretty cloth that has patterns of holes in it.
लेस/जालीदार गोटा
Her dress was dark blue with a white lace collar.

2 **Laces** are like pieces of string for fastening shoes.
जूते का फीता
He put on his shoes and tied the laces.

ladder *noun*
ladders

A **ladder** is a set of steps that you can move around. You use it for reaching high places.
सीढ़ी
He climbed the ladder to see over the wall.

lady *noun*
ladies

You can use **lady** to talk about a woman in a polite way.
महिला
She's a very nice old lady.

ladybird *noun*
ladybirds

A **ladybird** is a small round beetle that has red wings with black spots.
एक प्रकार का गुबरैला

laid
⇨ Look at **lay**.
She laid out the food on the table.

lain
⇨ Look at **lie**.
He had lain awake all night, worrying.

lake *noun*
lakes

A **lake** is an area of water with land around it.
झील

lamb *noun*
lambs

A **lamb** is a young sheep.
मेमना

lamp *noun*
lamps

A **lamp** is a light that uses electricity, oil or gas.
दीपक/कंदील
She turned on the lamp by her bed.

land *noun*

Land is an area of ground.
भूमि
This is good farm land.

land *verb*
lands, landing, landed

When something **lands**, it comes down to the ground after moving through the air.
ज़मीन पर उतरना
The ball landed in the middle of the road.

lane *noun*
lanes

A **lane** is a narrow road, usually in the country.
गली

language *noun*
languages

A **language** is a set of words that the people of a country use in talking or writing.
भाषा
*The English **language** has over 500,000 words.*

lap *noun*
laps

Your **lap** is the flat area on top of your thighs when you are sitting down.
गोद
*The boy sat on his dad's **lap**.*

large *adjective*
larger, largest

A **large** thing or person is big or bigger than usual.
बड़ा
*This fish lives in **large** rivers and lakes.*

last *adjective*

1   The **last** thing is the one before this one.
पिछला
*In the **last** lesson, we looked at some flowers.*

2   The **last** thing or person comes after all the others.
अंतिम
*I read the **last** three pages of the chapter.*

late
later, latest

1   **Late** means near the end of a period of time.
देर गए
*It was **late** in the afternoon.*

2   **Late** also means after the proper time.
विलंब से
*We arrived **late** for our class.*

laugh *verb*
laughs, laughing, laughed

When you **laugh**, you smile and make a sound because something is funny.
हँसना
*The boys all **laughed** at his joke.*

law *noun*
laws

A **law** is a rule that tells people what they may or may not do in a country.
कानून

lawn *noun*
lawns

A **lawn** is an area of short grass.
घास का मैदान
*Let's sit on the **lawn**.*

lay *verb*
lays, laying, laid

1   When you **lay** something somewhere, you put it down so that it lies there.
रखना
*   **Lay** the dishes on the table.*

2   When a bird **lays** an egg, it pushes an egg out of its body.
अंडे देना

lay

➡ Look at **lie**.
*We **lay** on the grass and looked at the sky.*

layer *noun*
layers

A **layer** is something that covers a surface, or that lies between two other things.
परत
*A **layer** of new snow covered the street.*

lazy *adjective*
lazier, laziest

A **lazy** person does not like working.
आलसी
*He was too **lazy** to read the whole book.*

lead *verb*
leads, leading, led

If you **lead** someone to a place, you take them there.
नेतृत्व करना/ले जाना
*I took his hand and started to **lead** him into the house.*

lead *noun*

If you are in the **lead** in a race or competition, you are winning.
आगे होना
*Our team was in the **lead** after ten minutes.*

lead *noun*

Lead is a soft, grey, heavy metal.
सीसा

leader *noun*
leaders

The **leader** of a group of people or a country is the person who is in charge of it.
नेता
*Your team **leaders** have your instructions.*

leaf *noun*
leaves

The **leaves** of a plant are the parts that are flat, thin, and usually green.
पत्ती
*A dry, brown **leaf** floated on the water.*

lean *verb*
leans, leaning, leant or **leaned**

When you **lean**, you bend your body from your waist.
झुकना/टेक लगाना
*She **leant** forwards and looked at me again.*

leap *verb*
leaps, leaping, leapt or **leaped**

If you **leap**, you jump a long way or very high.
छलाँग मारना
*He **leaped** in the air and waved his hands.*

learn *verb*
learns, learning, learnt or **learned**

When you **learn** something, you get to know it or how to do it.
सीखना
*When did you **learn** to swim?*

leather *noun*

Leather is the skin of some animals that you can use for making things.
चमड़ा
*Is your jacket made of real **leather**?*

leave *verb*
leaves, leaving, left

1 When you **leave** a place, you go away from it.
विदा होना/प्रस्थान करना
*Our bus **leaves** in an hour.*

2 If you **leave** something somewhere, you do not bring it with you.
छोड़ना
*I **left** my bags in the car.*

leaves

⇨ Look at **leaf**.
*The **leaves** are beginning to turn brown.*

led

⇨ Look at **lead**.
*The woman **led** me through the door into her office.*

left *noun*

The **left** is one side of something. For example, on a page, English writing begins on the **left**.
बायां भाग
*The school is on the **left** at the end of the road.*

left

⇨ Look at **leave**.
*The teacher suddenly **left** the room.*

leg noun
legs

1 A person's or animal's **legs** are the long parts of their body that they use for walking and standing.
टांग/पैर
Stand with your arms stretched out and your legs apart.

2 The **legs** of a table or chair are the long parts that it stands on.
पाया/गोड़ा
One of the legs is loose.

leg

lemon noun
lemons

A **lemon** is a yellow fruit with very sour juice.
नींबू

lend verb
lends, lending, lent

If you **lend** someone something, you give it to them for a period of time and then they give it back to you.
उधार देना
Will you lend me your pen?

length noun
lengths

The **length** of something is how long it is from one end to the other.
लंबाई
The table is about a metre in length.

lent

➡ Look at **lend**.
I lent her two books to read on holiday.

leopard noun
leopards

A **leopard** is a large, wild cat. **Leopards** have yellow fur with black spots, and live in Africa and Asia.
तेंदुआ

less adjective

Less means a smaller amount.
कम
I am trying to spend less money on sweets.

lesson noun
lessons

A **lesson** is a period of time when someone teaches you something.
पाठ
My sister has a piano lesson every Monday.

let verb
lets, letting, let

1 If you **let** someone do something, you allow them to do it.
अनुमति देना

2 You can say **let's** when you want someone to do something with you. **Let's** is short for **let us**.
चलो
Let's go!

letter noun
letters

1 A **letter** is a message on paper that you post to someone.
पत्र
I received a letter from a friend.

2 **Letters** are shapes that you write to make words.
अक्षर
The children practised writing the letters in class.

lettuce noun
lettuces

A **lettuce** is a vegetable with large green leaves that you eat in salads.
सलाद का पत्ता

library noun
libraries

A **library** is a place where you can go to read or borrow books.
पुस्तकालय
I'm going to the library to look for a book about whales.

lick verb
licks, licking, licked

If you **lick** something, you move your tongue over it.
चाटना
Lick the stamp before you put it on the envelope.

A
B
C
D
E
F
G
H
I
J
K
L
M
N
O
P
Q
R
S
T
U
V
W
X
Y
Z

lid noun
lids

A **lid** is the top of a container that you can remove.
ढक्कन
She lifted the lid of the box.

lie verb
lies, lying, lay, lain

When you **lie** somewhere, your body is flat, and you are not standing or sitting.
लेटना
Lie on the bed and close your eyes for a while.

lie noun
lies

A **lie** is something you say that is not true.
झूठ
You told me a lie!

life noun
lives

Your **life** is the period of time when you are alive.
जीवन
I want to live here for the rest of my life.

lift verb
lifts, lifting, lifted

When you **lift** something, you take it and move it up.
उठाना
He lifted the bag on to his shoulder.

light noun
lights

1 **Light** is the bright energy that comes from the sun, that lets you see things.
प्रकाश
A little light comes into the room through the thin curtains.

2 A **light** is something like a lamp, that allows you to see.
प्रकाश
There was only one small light in the room.

light adjective
lighter, lightest

1 If a place is **light**, it is bright because of the sun or lamps.
प्रकाशमय/उजाला
It gets light at about 6 o' clock here.

2 Something that is **light** is not heavy.
हलका
The chair is quite light so we can move it if we want to.

3 A **light** colour is pale.
हल्का
His shirt was light blue.

light verb
lights, lighting, lit

When you **light** a fire, it starts burning.
जलाना
We used a whole box of matches to light the fire.

lightning noun

Lightning is the very bright flashes of light in the sky in a storm.
तड़ित
There was thunder and lightning and big black clouds in the sky.

like

1 If things or people are **like** each other, they are almost the same.
के समान
He's very funny, like my uncle.

2 You say what something or someone is **like** when you are talking about how they seem to you.
सदृश/जैसा
"What was the party like?"—"Oh it was great!"

like verb
likes, liking, liked

If you **like** something, you think it is nice or interesting.
पसंद करना
Do you like swimming?

a b c d e f g h i j k l m n o p q r s t u v w x y z

line *noun*
lines

A **line** is a long, thin mark or shape.
रेखा
Draw a line at the bottom of the page.

lion *noun*
lions

A **lion** is a large wild cat that lives in Africa. **Lions** have yellow fur, and male **lions** have long hair on their head and neck.
शेर

lip *noun*
lips

Your **lips** are the edges of your mouth.
होंठ
He bit his lip.

liquid *noun*
liquids

A **liquid** is something that you can pour. Water and oil are **liquids**.
तरल
The bottle is full of clear liquid.

list *noun*
lists

A **list** is a set of names or other things that you write one below the other.
सूची
There are six names on the list.

listen *verb*
listens, listening, listened

If you **listen** to something, you hear it and give it your attention.
ध्यान से सुनना
He's listening to the radio.

lit
➡ Look at **light**.
He took a match and lit the candle.

litre *noun*
litres

A **litre** is used for measuring liquid.
लीटर

litter *noun*
Litter is rubbish that people drop in the street.
कूड़ा
Please don't drop any litter.

little *adjective*
littler, littlest

A person or thing that is **little** is small in size.
छोटा
They live in a little house.

live *verb*
lives, living, lived

1 You **live** in the place where your home is.
रहना
Where do you live?

2 To **live** means to be alive.
जीना/जीवित रहना
We all need water to live.

lives
➡ Look at **life**.
Their lives were changed.

lizard *noun*
lizards

A **lizard** is a small reptile with a long tail and rough skin.
छिपकली

load *verb*
loads, loading, loaded

If you **load** a vehicle, you put something on it.
लादना
We finished loading the bags on to the lorry.

loaf *noun*
loaves

A **loaf** is bread that you cut into slices.
पावरोटी

*He bought a **loaf** of bread and some cheese.*

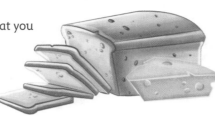

lock *verb*
locks, locking, locked

When you **lock** a door, you close it with a key.
ताला लगाना

*Are you sure you **locked** the front door?*

log *noun*
logs

A **log** is a thick piece of wood from a tree.
लट्ठा/कुंदा

*We sat around a **log** fire.*

lolly *noun*
lollies

A **lolly** is a sweet or ice cream on a stick.
लॉलीपॉप

long *adjective*
longer, longest

1   Something that is **long** takes a lot of time.
    लंबा

    *The afternoon lessons seemed very **long**.*

2   Something that is **long** measures a great distance from one end to the other.
    लंबा

    *There is a **long** table in the middle of the kitchen.*

look *verb*
looks, looking, looked

1   When you **look** at something, you turn your eyes so that you can see it.
    देखना

    *I **looked** at the clock and yawned.*

2   You use **look** when you describe how a person seems.
    दिखाई देना

    *The little girl **looked** sad.*

loose *adjective*
looser, loosest

1   Something that is **loose** moves when it should not.
    शिथिल/ढीला

    *One of the table legs is **loose**.*

2   **Loose** clothes are rather large and are not tight.
    ढीला

    *Wear **loose**, comfortable clothes when you do the exercises.*

lorry *noun*
lorries

A **lorry** is a large vehicle for moving things by road.
मालवाहक गाड़ी

lose *verb*
loses, losing, lost

1   If you **lose** a game, you do not win it.
    हारना

    *Our team **lost** the match by one point.*

2   If you **lose** something, you do not know where it is.
    खो देना

    *I've **lost** my keys.*

lost *adjective*

If you are **lost**, you do not know where you are.
गुम

*I suddenly knew that I was **lost**.*

lot *or* lots

A **lot** of something, or **lots** of something, is a large amount of it.
ढेर सारा

*He drank **lots** of milk.*

loud *adjective*
louder, loudest

A **loud** noise is a very big sound.
तीव्र

*The music was very **loud**.*

a
b
c
d
e
f
g
h
i
j
k
l
m
n
o
p
q
r
s
t
u
v
w
x
y
z

love *verb*
loves, loving, loved

1 If you **love** someone, you care very much about them.
प्यार करना

2 If you **love** something, you like it very much.
पसंद करना
*We both **love** football.*

lovely *adjective*
lovelier, loveliest

A **lovely** thing or person is very beautiful or very nice.
मनोहर/सुंदर
*I thought she looked **lovely**.*

low *adjective*
lower, lowest

1 Something that is **low** is close to the ground.
नीचा
*There is a **low** fence around the house.*

2 A **low** number is a small number.
कम/निम्न
*The price was very **low**.*

lucky *adjective*
luckier, luckiest

Someone who is **lucky** enjoys good things that people don't expect to happen.
भाग्यशाली
*He was **lucky** to win the competition.*

lump *noun*
lumps

A **lump** is a solid piece of something.
ढेला/डली
*There was a bowl full of **lumps** of sugar.*

lunch *noun*
lunches

Lunch is the meal that you have in the middle of the day.
दोपहर का भोजन

lying
⇨ Look at **lie**.
*There was a man **lying** on the ground.*

machine *noun*
machines

A **machine** is a piece of equipment that uses electricity or an engine to do something.
मशीन/यंत्र
*I left a message on the answering **machine**.*

made
⇨ Look at **make**.
*Mum **made** me a big birthday cake.*

magazine *noun*
magazines

A **magazine** is a thin book with stories and pictures in it.
पत्रिका
*I get my favourite **magazine** every Thursday.*

magic *noun*

In stories, **magic** is a special power that allows you to do impossible things.
जादू
*By **magic**, the man turned to stone.*

magnet *noun*
magnets

A **magnet** is a piece of metal that attracts iron towards it.
चुंबक

main *adjective*

The **main** thing is the most important one.
मुख्य
*That's the **main** reason I want it.*

make *verb*
makes, making, made

1 If you **make** something, you put it together or build it from other things.
बनाना
*She **makes** all her own clothes.*

2 You can use **make** to show that a person does or says something.
करना
*He **made** a phone call.*

3 If you **make** a person do something, they must do it.
मजबूर करना
*Mum **made** me clean the bathroom.*

male *adjective*

A **male** person or animal could become a father.
नर/पुरुष
*All of the pupils were **male**.*

mammal *noun*
mammals

Mammals are animals that feed their babies with milk.
स्तनधारी प्राणी
*Some **mammals**, like whales, live in the sea.*

man *noun*
men

A **man** is an adult male person.
मर्द
*The book is for both **men** and women.*

manage *verb*
manages, managing, managed

If you **manage** something, you control it.
प्रबंधन करना
*He **managed** the bank for 20 years.*

many *adjective*

If there are **many** people or things, there are a lot of them.
कई
*Does he have **many** friends?*

map *noun*
maps

A **map** is a drawing of an area from above. It shows where the roads, rivers and railways are.
मानचित्र
*You can see the park beside this road on the **map**.*

March *noun*

March is the month after February and before April. It has 31 days.
मार्च

mark *noun*
marks

1 A **mark** is a small dirty area on a surface.
दाग़
*I can't get this **mark** off my shirt.*

2 A **mark** is a shape that you write or draw.
निशान
*He made a few **marks** with his pen.*

market *noun*
markets

A **market** is a place where people buy and sell things.
बाज़ार
*There's a **market** in the town centre every Saturday morning.*

marmalade *noun*

Marmalade is jam that is made from oranges.
एक प्रकार का मुरब्बा

marry *verb*
marries, marrying, married

When a man and a woman **marry**, they become husband and wife.
विवाह करना

mask *noun*
masks

A **mask** is something that you wear over your face to protect or hide it.
मुखौटा

a
b
c
d
e
f
g
h
i
j
k
l
m
n
o
p
q
r
s
t
u
v
w
x
y
z

A B C D E F G H I J K L **M** N O P Q R S T U V W X Y Z

mat *noun*
mats

A **mat** is a small piece of cloth, wood, or plastic that you put on a table to protect it.
चटाई
*I put my glass on a red **mat**.*

match *noun*
matches

1 A **match** is a small, thin stick that makes a flame when you rub it on a rough surface.
माचिस
*She lit a **match** and held it up to the candle.*

2 A **match** is a game of football, cricket, or some other sport.
खेल प्रतियोगिता
*We won all our **matches** last year.*

match *verb*
matches, matching, matched

If one thing **matches** another, they look good together.
मेल खाना
*Do these shoes **match** my dress?*

material *noun*
materials

1 **Material** is cloth.
कपड़ा
*Her skirt was made from thick black **material**.*

2 A **material** is what something is made of, like rock, glass or plastic.
सामग्री/पदार्थ
*Wax is a soft **material**.*

maths *noun*

If you learn **maths**, you learn about numbers, shapes, and amounts.
गणित

matter *verb*
matters, mattered

If something **matters** to you, it is important.
फ़र्क पड़ना/महत्वपूर्ण होना
*Never mind, it doesn't **matter**.*

may *verb*

1 If you **may** do something, it is possible that you will do it.
हो सकना
*I **may** come back next year.*

2 If you **may** do something, you can do it because someone allows you to do it.
कर सकना
*Please **may** I leave the room?*

May *noun*

May is the month after April and before June. It has 31 days.
मई

me

You use **me** when you are talking about yourself.
मुझे
*Can you hear **me**?*

meal *noun*
meals

A **meal** is food that you eat at one time. Breakfast, lunch and dinner are **meals**.
भोजन
*She sat next to me for every **meal**.*

mean *verb*
means, meaning, meant

1 If you ask what something **means**, you want to understand it.
मतलब होना
*What does this word **mean**?*

2 If you **mean** what you are saying, it is not a joke.
मायने रखना
*He says he loves her, and I think he **means** it.*

3 If you **mean** to do something, it is not an accident.
अभिप्राय रखना/इरादा रखना
*I didn't **mean** to drop the cup.*

mean *adjective*
meaner, meanest

Someone who is **mean** is not nice to other people.
अनुदार/घटिया
*He was sorry for being **mean** to her.*

measles *noun*

Measles is an illness that gives you a fever and red spots on your skin.
खसरा

measure *verb*
measures, measuring, measured

If you **measure** something, you find its size.
मापना
*First **measure** the length of the table.*

meat *noun*

Meat is the part of an animal that people cook and eat.
मांस
*I don't eat **meat** or fish.*

medicine *noun*

Medicine is something that you swallow to make you better when you are ill.
दवा
*The **medicine** saved his life.*

meet *verb*
meets, meeting, met

If you **meet** someone, you see them and you talk to them.
मिलना/मुलाकात करना
*I **met** my friends in town today.*

melon *noun*
melons

A **melon** is a large, soft, sweet fruit with a hard green or yellow skin.
खरबूज/तरबूज़
*We ate slices of **melon**.*

melt *verb*
melts, melting, melted

When something **melts**, it changes from a solid to a liquid as it becomes warmer.
पिघलना
Melt the chocolate in a bowl.

memory *noun*
memories

1 Your **memory** is the part of your mind that remembers things.
स्मरणशक्ति/याद्दाश्त
*He has a very good **memory** for numbers.*

2 A **memory** is something you remember about the past.
याद/स्मृति
*They discussed their **memories** of their school days.*

men

⇨ Look at **man**.
*He ordered his **men** to stop.*

mend *verb*
mends, mending, mended

If you **mend** something that is broken, you repair it.
मरम्मत करना
*They **mended** the hole in the roof.*

mess *noun*

If something is a **mess**, it is not neat.
गंदगी
*After the party, the house was a **mess**.*

message *noun*
messages

A **message** is a piece of information that you send someone.
संदेश
*I got emails and **messages** from friends all over the world.*

messy *adjective*
messier, messiest

A person or thing that is **messy** is not neat.
गंदा
*His writing is rather **messy**.*

met

⇨ Look at **meet**.
*We **met** when we were on holiday.*

a
b
c
d
e
f
g
h
i
j
k
l
m
n
o
p
q
r
s
t
u
v
w
x
y
z

A
B
C
D
E
F
G
H
I
J
K
L
M
N
O
P
Q
R
S
T
U
V
W
X
Y
Z

metal *noun*
metals

Metal is a hard material that melts when it gets very hot.
धातु
Gold, iron and lead are different kinds of metal.

metre *noun*
metres

A **metre** is used for measuring distances or how long things are.
मीटर
The hole in the ground is about one and a half metres across.

mice

⇨ Look at **mouse**.
You can hear the mice under the floor.

midday *noun*

Midday is twelve o'clock in the middle of the day.
मध्याह्न
At midday everyone had lunch.

middle *noun*
middles

The **middle** of something is the part that is the same distance from each edge or end.
मध्य
We stood in the middle of the room.

midnight *noun*

Midnight is twelve o'clock at night.
मध्यरात्रि
They went to bed after midnight.

might *verb*

You use **might** when something is possible.
हो सकना
He might win the race.

mile *noun*
miles

A **mile** is used for measuring distance.
मील
They drove 600 miles across the desert.

milk *noun*

Milk is the white liquid that all baby mammals get from their mothers. People also drink **milk** that farmers get from cows.
दूध
They make cheese from goat's and sheep's milk too.

millilitre *noun*
millilitres

A **millilitre** is used for measuring liquid. There are 1,000 **millilitres** in a litre.
मिलीलीटर
I gave him the medicine with a 5 millilitre spoon.

millimetre *noun*
millimetres

A **millimetre** is used for measuring how long things are. There are 1,000 **millimetres** in a metre.
मिलिमीटर
The small insect was a few millimetres long.

mind *noun*
minds

Your **mind** is the part of your brain that thinks, understands and remembers.
मस्तिष्क
I can't get that song out of my mind.

mind *verb*
minds, minding, minded

If you **mind** something, it annoys you.
बुरा मानना/आपत्ति करना
It was hard work but she didn't mind.

mine

Mine means belonging to me.
मेरा
That isn't your bag, it's mine.

mine *noun*
mines

A **mine** is a deep hole or tunnel where people go to dig things like gold or diamonds out of rock.
खदान/खान

minus

You use **minus** when you take one number away from another number.
घटाव

*Three **minus** two is one.*

minute *noun*
minutes

A **minute** is used for measuring time. There are sixty seconds in one **minute**.
मिनट

*The food will take 20 **minutes** to cook.*

minute *adjective*

Something that is **minute** is very small.
छोटा/बारीक

*You only need to use a **minute** amount of glue.*

miss *verb*
misses, missing, missed

1 If you **miss** something that you are trying to hit or catch, you do not manage to hit it or catch it.
चूक जाना
   *I jumped, but **missed** the ball.*

2 If you **miss** something, you do not notice it.
देखने में असफल होना/चूकना
   *What did he say? I **missed** it.*

3 If you **miss** someone who is not with you, you feel sad that they are not there.
कमी महसूस करना
   *The boys **miss** their father.*

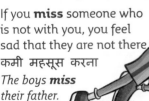

Miss

You use **Miss** in front of the name of a girl or a woman who is not married when you are talking to her or talking about her.
कुमारी

*Do you know **Miss** Smith?*

mistake *noun*
mistakes

A **mistake** is something that is not correct.
ग़लती

*I made three **mistakes** in my letter.*

mix *verb*
mixes, mixing, mixed

If you **mix** things, you put different things together to make something new.
मिलाना/मिश्रित करना

***Mix** the sugar with the butter.*

mixture *noun*
mixtures

A **mixture** is what you make when you mix different things together.
मिश्रण

*The drink is a **mixture** of orange and apple juice.*

mobile phone *noun*
mobile phones

A **mobile phone** is a small phone that you can take everywhere with you.
मोबाइल फ़ोन

model *noun*
models

1 A **model** is a small copy of something.
नमूना
   *I made the **model** house with paper and glue.*

2 A **model** is a person whose job is to wear and show new clothes.
मॉडल
   *The **model** in the picture was very tall.*

mole *noun*
moles

1 A **mole** is a natural dark spot on your skin.
तिल
   *She has a **mole** on the side of her nose.*

2 A **mole** is a small animal with black fur that lives under the ground.
छछूंदर

A B C D E F G H I J K L **M** N O P Q R S T U V W X Y Z

moment *noun*
moments

A **moment** is a very short period of time.
क्षण
He stopped for a moment.

Monday *noun*
Mondays

Monday is the day after Sunday and before Tuesday.
सोमवार
I went back to school on Monday.

money *noun*

Money is what you use to buy things.
धन
Cars cost a lot of money.

monkey *noun*
monkeys

A **monkey** is an animal that has a long tail and can climb trees.
बंदर

monster *noun*
monsters

In stories, a **monster** is a big, ugly creature that frightens people.
राक्षस
The film is about a monster in the wardrobe.

month *noun*
months

A **month** is one part of a year. There are twelve **months** in one year.
महीना
We are going on holiday next month.

moon *noun*
moons

The **moon** shines in the sky at night and moves around the earth every month.
चंद्रमा
The first man on the moon was Neil Armstrong.

more

You use **more** to talk about a greater amount of something.
ज़्यादा/अधिक
He has more chips than me.

morning *noun*
mornings

The **morning** is the early part of the day, before lunch.
सुबह
What do you want to do tomorrow morning?

most

1 **Most** of a group of things or people means nearly all of them.
ज़्यादातर/अधिकतर
Most of the houses here are very old.

2 The **most** means the largest amount.
सर्वाधिक
Who has the most money?

moth *noun*
moths

A **moth** is an insect like a butterfly that usually flies at night.
शलभ

mother *noun*
mothers

A **mother** is a woman who has a child.
माँ

motorbike *noun*
motorbikes

A **motorbike** is a large bike with an engine.
मोटरसाइकिल

motorway noun
motorways

A **motorway** is a wide road for travelling long distances fast.
चौड़ा मार्ग

mountain noun
mountains

A **mountain** is a very high area of land with steep sides.
पर्वत

*Ben Nevis is the highest **mountain** in Scotland.*

mouse noun
mice

1 A **mouse** is a small animal with a long tail.
चूहा

2 You use a **mouse** to move things on a computer screen.
माउस

mouth noun
mouths

Your **mouth** is the part of your face that you use for eating or talking.
मुँह

*When you cough, please cover your **mouth**.*

move verb
moves, moving, moved

1 When you **move** something, you put it in a different place.
हटाना

*The man asked her to **move** her car.*

2 If you **move**, you go to live in a different place.
हटना/जगह बदलना

*She's **moving** to London next month.*

Mr

You use **Mr** before a man's name when you are talking to him or talking about him.
श्री

*Our history teacher's name is **Mr** Jones.*

Mrs

You use **Mrs** before a married woman's name when you are talking to her or talking about her.
श्रीमती

*How are you, **Mrs** Smith?*

Ms

You use **Ms** before a woman's name when you are talking to her or talking about her.
कुमार

*The message is for **Ms** Clark.*

much

You use **much** to talk about a large amount of something.
बहुत

*I ate too **much** food.*

mud noun

Mud is a mixture of earth and water.
कीचड़

*There was thick **mud** on my football boots.*

muddy adjective
muddier, muddiest

If something is **muddy**, it is covered with mud.
कीचड़ भरा

*My boots are all **muddy**!*

mug noun
mugs

A **mug** is a deep cup with straight sides.
प्याला/मग

*He poured tea into the **mugs**.*

a
b
c
d
e
f
g
h
i
j
k
l
m
n
o
p
q
r
s
t
u
v
w
x
y
z

A B C D E F G H I J K L **M** N O P Q R S T U V W X Y Z

multiplication *noun*

Multiplication is when you multiply one number by another.
गुणन

multiply *verb*
multiplies, multiplying, multiplied

If you **multiply** a number, you add it to itself a number of times.
गुणा करना
*You get 24 if you **multiply** three by eight.*

mum or mummy *noun*
mums or mummies

Mum or **mummy** is a name for your mother.
माँ

muscle *noun*
muscles

Your **muscles** are the parts inside your body that help you move.
मांसपेशी
*Sport helps to keep your **muscles** strong.*

museum *noun*
museums

A **museum** is a building where you can look at interesting, old, and valuable things.
अजायबघर
*Hundreds of people came to the **museum** to see the dinosaur bones.*

mushroom *noun*
mushrooms

A **mushroom** is a plant with a short stem and a round top that you can eat.
कुकुरमुत्ता
*There are many types of wild **mushroom**, and some of them are poisonous.*

music *noun*

Music is the sound that you make when you sing or play instruments.
संगीत
*What's your favourite **music**?*

musical instrument *noun*
musical instruments

A **musical instrument** is an instrument that you use to play music, like a piano or a guitar.
साज़/वाद्ययंत्र

must *verb*

You use **must** to show that you think something is very important.
आवश्यक होना
*You **must** tell the police all the facts.*

mustn't

Mustn't is short for **must not**.
बिलकुल नहीं करना चाहिए'
*I **mustn't** forget to take my key with me.*

my

You use **my** to show that something belongs to you.
अपना/मेरा
*I went to sleep in **my** room.*

myself

You use **myself** when the you are talking about yourself.
स्वयं
*I hurt **myself** when I fell down.*

mystery *noun*
mysteries

A **mystery** is something that you do not understand or know about.
रहस्य
*Why she's crying is a **mystery**.*

myth *noun*
myths

A **myth** is a very old story about magic, and strange people and creatures.
मिथक

Nn

nail *noun*
nails

1 A **nail** is a thin piece of metal. It is flat at one end and it has a point at the other end.
कील
*A picture hung on a **nail** in the wall.*

2 Your **nails** are the thin hard parts that grow at the ends of your fingers and toes.
नाखून
*Try to keep your **nails** short.*

name *noun*
names

A person's **name** is the word or words that you use to talk to them, or to talk about them.
नाम
*Is your **name** Peter?*

narrow *adjective*
narrower, narrowest

Something that is **narrow** is a small distance from one side to the other.
सँकरा
*We walked through the town's **narrow** streets.*

nasty *adjective*
nastier, nastiest

Something that is **nasty** is horrible.
खराब
*That's a **nasty** thing to say!*

natural *adjective*

Natural things come from nature.
प्राकृतिक
*The **natural** home of these animals is under the ground.*

nature *noun*

Nature is all the animals, plants, and other things in the world that people did not make or change.
प्रकृति
*We watched **nature** all around us from our camp in the forest.*

naughty *adjective*
naughtier, naughtiest

A **naughty** child does things which are bad.
शरारती
*She was so **naughty**, her mother sent her to bed early.*

near *adjective*
nearer, nearest

If something is **near** a place, thing, or person, it is not far away from them.
पास/समीप
*We are very **near** my house.*

nearly

Nearly means almost.
लगभग
*It's **nearly** five o'clock.*

neat *adjective*
neater, neatest

A **neat** place or person is clean and tidy.
साफ
*She made sure that her room was **neat** before she left.*

neck *noun*
necks

Your **neck** is the part of your body between your head and the rest of your body.
गरदन
*He wore a gold chain around his **neck**.*

a
b
c
d
e
f
g
h
i
j
k
l
m
n
o
p
q
r
s
t
u
v
w
x
y
z

necklace *noun*
necklaces

A **necklace** is a chain of beads or jewels that you wear around your neck.
हार
*She's wearing a beautiful **necklace**.*

need *verb*
needs, needing, needed

If you **need** something, you believe that you must have it or do it.
ज़रूरत होना
*I **need** some more money.*

needle *noun*
needles

A **needle** is a small, thin metal tool with a sharp point that you use for sewing.
सूई
*If you get me a **needle** and thread, I'll sew the button on.*

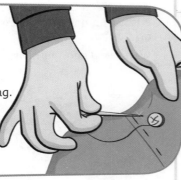

needn't

Needn't is short for **need not**.
की ज़रूरत नहीं
*You **needn't** come with us if you don't want to.*

neighbour *noun*
neighbours

Your **neighbours** are the people who live around you.
पड़ोसी
*I met our **neighbour** when I went to the shops.*

nephew *noun*
nephews

Someone's **nephew** is the son of their sister or brother.
भतीजा/भांजा
*I have a **nephew** who is still a baby.*

nervous *adjective*

If you are **nervous** about something, it worries you and you are rather afraid.
घबराया हुआ
*I tried not to show that I was **nervous**.*

nest *noun*
nests

A **nest** is the place where a bird keeps its eggs or its babies.
घोंसला
*There were six small eggs in the bird's **nest**.*

net *noun*
nets

A **net** is made from pieces of string or rope tied together with holes between them. It is for catching things like fish, or the ball in some sports.
जाल
*The idea is to throw the ball into the top of the **net**.*

never

Never means at no time in the past, present or future.
कभी नहीं
***Never** look straight at the sun.*

new *adjective*
newer, newest

1   Something that is **new** was not there before.
    नया
    *They discovered a **new** medicine for his illness.*

2   If something is **new**, nobody has used it before.
    नया
    *I am wearing my **new** shoes.*

3   A **new** thing or person is a different one from the one you had before.
    नया
    *We have a **new** history teacher.*

news *noun*

News is information that you did not know before.
समाचार
*We waited and waited for **news** of him.*

newspaper *noun*
newspapers

A **newspaper** is a number of large sheets of paper with news and other information printed on them.
समाचारपत्र
*They read about it in the **newspaper**.*

next *adjective*

The **next** thing is the one that comes immediately after this one or after the last one.
अगला
*I got up early the **next** morning.*

nice *adjective*
nicer, nicest

If something is **nice**, you like it.
बढ़िया/अच्छा
*They live in a really **nice** house.*

niece *noun*
nieces

Someone's **niece** is the daughter of their sister or brother.
भतीजी/भांजी
*He bought a present for his **niece**.*

night *noun*
nights

The **night** is the time when it is dark outside, and most people sleep.
रात
*It's eleven o'clock at **night** in Beijing.*

nightdress *noun*
nightdresses

A **nightdress** is a loose dress that a woman or girl can wear to sleep in.
रात्रिकालीन पोशाक

nightmare *noun*
nightmares

A **nightmare** is a dream that frightens or worries you.
दुःस्वप्न
*She had a **nightmare** last night.*

nine

Nine is the number .
नौ

no

You use **no** to say that something is not true or to refuse something.
नहीं
*"Would you like a drink?"—"**No** thank you."*

nobody *noun*

Nobody means not one person.
कोई नहीं
*For a long time, **nobody** spoke.*

nod *verb*
nods, nodding, nodded

When you **nod**, you move your head up and down, usually to show that you agree.
सिर हिलाना/सहमति प्रकट करना
*She **nodded** and smiled.*

noise *noun*
noises

A **noise** is a loud sound.
शोर
*Suddenly there was a **noise** like thunder.*

noisy *adjective*
noisier, noisiest

A **noisy** person or thing makes a lot of loud noise.
शोरगुल वाला
*It was a very **noisy** party.*

none

None means not one or not any.
कोई भी नहीं
***None** of us knew her.*

nonsense *noun*

If something is **nonsense**, it is not true or it is silly.
बकवास
*My father said the story was **nonsense**.*

noon *noun*

Noon is twelve o'clock in the middle of the day.
दोपहर
*The lesson started at **noon**.*

north *noun*

The **north** is the direction to your left when you are looking towards the place where the sun rises.
उत्तर दिशा

nose *noun*
noses

Your **nose** is the part of your face above your mouth that you use for breathing and for noticing smells.
नाक
*She sneezed and blew her **nose**.*

nostril *noun*
nostrils

Your **nostrils** are the two holes at the end of your nose.
नथुना
*Keeping your mouth closed, breathe in through your **nostrils**.*

note *noun*
notes

1 A **note** is a short letter or message.
छोटी चिट्ठी/टिप्पणी
*He wrote her a **note** and left it on the table.*

2 A **note** is one musical sound.
सुर
*She played some **notes** on her recorder.*

nothing

Nothing means not anything.
कुछ नहीं
*There was **nothing** to do.*

notice *verb*
notices, noticing, noticed

If you **notice** something, you suddenly see or hear it.
ध्यान देना
*Did you **notice** him leave the room?*

notice *noun*
notices

A **notice** is a sign that gives information or instructions.
सूचना पत्र
*The **notice** said "Please close the door."*

noun *noun*
nouns

A **noun** is a word that is used for talking about a person or thing. Examples of **nouns** are "child", "table", "sun", and "strength".
संज्ञा

November *noun*

November is the month after October and before December. It has 30 days.
नवंबर

now

You use **now** to talk about the present time.
अब
*I must go **now**.*

nowhere

Nowhere means not anywhere.
कहीं नहीं
*There's **nowhere** quiet for me to do my homework.*

number *noun*
numbers

A **number** is a word that you use to count.
अंक
*What **number** is your house?*

nurse *noun*
nurses

A **nurse** is a person whose job is to care for people who are ill.
नर्स
*She thanked the **nurses** at the hospital.*

nut *noun*
nuts

A **nut** is a dry fruit with a hard shell.
कड़े छिलके वाले मेवे या फल
Nuts and seeds are very good for you.

A B C D E F G H I J K L M N O P Q R S T U V W X Y Z

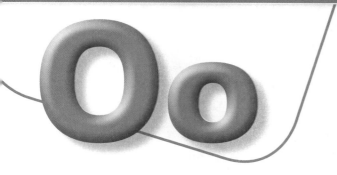

oak *noun*
oaks

An **oak** tree is a big, tall tree with a wide trunk. Its wood is good for making furniture.
शाहबलूत का वृक्ष

oar *noun*
oars

An **oar** is a long piece of wood with a wide, flat end, used for moving a boat through the water.
पतवार

obey *verb*
obeys, obeying, obeyed

If you **obey** a person or an order, you do what you are told to do.
आज्ञा पालन

ocean *noun*
oceans

An **ocean** is a big sea.
महासागर
We crossed the Atlantic Ocean.

o'clock *noun*

You say **o'clock** when saying what time it is.
बजे
It is eight o'clock in the morning.

octagon *noun*
octagons

An **octagon** is a shape with eight straight sides.
अष्टभुज

October *noun*

October is the month after September and before November. It has 31 days.
अक्तूबर

octopus *noun*
octopuses

An **octopus** is a soft ocean animal with eight long arms.
ऑक्टोपस

odd *adjective*
odder, oddest

1 If something is **odd**, it is strange or unusual.
अजीब
There was an odd smell in the kitchen.

2 You say that two things are **odd** when they do not belong to the same set or pair.
बेमेल
I'm wearing odd socks.

3 **Odd** numbers, such as 3 and 17, are numbers that cannot be divided by the number two.
विषम

off

1 If you take something **off** another thing, it is no longer on it.
पर से
He took his feet off the desk.

2 When something that uses electricity is **off**, it is not using electricity.
बंद
The light was off.

offer *verb*
offers, offering, offered

If you **offer** something to someone, you ask them if they would like to have it.
प्रदान करना/देना
He offered his seat to the young woman.

A
B
C
D
E
F
G
H
I
J
K
L
M
N
O
P
Q
R
S
T
U
V
W
X
Y
Z

office *noun*
offices

An **office** is a room where people work at desks.
कार्यालय

often

Something that happens **often** happens many times or a lot of the time.
अक्सर

oil *noun*

Oil is a thick liquid.
तेल
We need some cooking oil.

old *adjective*
older, oldest

1 An **old** person is someone who has lived for a long time.
वृद्ध
An old lady sat next to me.

2 An **old** thing is something that somebody made a long time ago.
पुराना
We have a very old car.

on

1 If someone or something is **on** a surface, it is resting there.
पर/के ऊपर
There was a large box on the table.

2 When something that uses electricity is **on**, it is using electricity.
चालू
The television is on.

once

If something happens **once**, it happens one time only.
एक बार
I met her once, at a party.

one *noun*

One is the number **1**.
संख्या एक

onion *noun*
onions

An **onion** is a small, round vegetable with a brown skin like paper and a very strong taste.
प्याज़

only

1 If you talk about the **only** thing or person, you mean that there are no others.
एकमात्र/केवल
It was the only shop in the town.

2 You use **only** when you are saying how small or short something is.
केवल
Their house is only a few miles from here.

3 If you are an **only** child, you have no brothers or sisters.
इकलौता

open *verb*
opens, opening, opened

1 When you **open** something, or when it **opens**, you move it so that it is no longer closed.
खोलना/खुलना
She opened the door.

2 When a shop or office **opens**, people are able to go in.
खुलना
The banks will open again on Monday morning.

opposite

1 If one thing is **opposite** another, it is across from it.
सम्मुख
Jennie sat opposite Sam at breakfast.

2 If things are **opposite**, they are as different as they can be.
विपरीत/उलटा
We watched the cars driving in the opposite direction.

orange *noun*

1 An **orange** is a round fruit with a thick skin and lots of juice.
संतरा

2 **Orange** is a colour between red and yellow.
नारंगी रंग
Tigers are orange with black stripes.

orchestra *noun*
orchestras

An **orchestra** is a large group of people who play music together.
वादक मंडली
The orchestra began to play.

order *verb*
orders, ordering, ordered

If you **order** someone to do something, you tell them to do it.
आज्ञा देना
*She **ordered** him to leave.*

ordinary *adjective*

Ordinary means not special or different in any way.
साधारण
*It was just an **ordinary** day.*

other *adjective*
others

Other people or things are different people or things.
अन्य
*All the **other** children had gone home.*

our

You use **our** to show that something belongs to you and one or more other people.
हमारा
***Our** house is near the school.*

ours

You use **ours** when you are talking about something that belongs to you and one or more other people.
हमारा
*That car is **ours**.*

out

1 If you go **out** of a place, you leave it.
बाहर
*She ran **out** of the house.*

2 If you are **out**, you are not at home.
घर से बाहर
*I called you yesterday, but you were **out**.*

3 If a light is **out**, it is no longer shining.
बुझा हुआ
*All the lights were **out** in the house.*

outside

1 The **outside** of something is the part that covers the rest of it.
बाहरी भाग
*They are painting the **outside** of the building.*

2 If you are **outside**, you are not in a building.
बाहर
*Let's play **outside**.*

oval *adjective*

Oval things have a shape like an egg.
अंडाकार
*She has an **oval** table.*

oven *noun*
ovens

An **oven** is the part of a cooker like a large metal box with a door.
तंदूर/भट्ठी

over

1 If one thing is **over** another thing, the first thing is above or higher than the second thing.
के ऊपर
*There was a lamp **over** the table.*

2 If something is **over**, it has finished.
समाप्त
*The class is **over**.*

owe *verb*
owes, owing, owed

If you **owe** money to someone, you have to pay money to them.
ऋणी होना
*He **owes** him $50.*

owl *noun*
owls

An **owl** is a bird with large eyes that hunts at night.
उल्लू

own

You use **own** to say that something belongs to you.
अपना/खुद का
*Jennifer wanted her **own** room.*

ox *noun*
oxen

An **ox** is a kind of bull that is used for carrying or pulling things.
बैल

pack *verb*
packs, packing, packed
When you **pack** a bag, you put clothes and other things into it, because you are going away.
सामान बाँधना

paddle *noun*
paddles
A **paddle** is a short oar. You use it to move a small boat through water.
डाँड/पतवार

paddle *verb*
paddles, paddling, paddled
1 If someone **paddles** a boat, they move it using a paddle.
नाव खेना/डांड चलाना
2 If you **paddle**, you walk in shallow water.
छिछले पानी में चलना

page *noun*
pages
A **page** is one side of a piece of paper in a book, a magazine, or a newspaper.
पृष्ठ
*Turn to **page** 4.*

paid
⇨ Look at **pay**.
*Daddy **paid** for the sweets.*

pain *noun*
pains
Pain is the feeling that you have in a part of your body, because of illness or an accident.
दर्द
*I felt a sudden sharp **pain** in my ankle.*

painful *adjective*
If a part of your body is **painful**, it hurts.
दर्दनाक
*His right knee is very **painful**.*

paint *noun*
paints
Paint is a liquid used to decorate buildings, or to make a picture.
रंग
*Can I use some of your red **paint**?*

paint *verb*
paints, painting, painted
1 If you **paint** something on a piece of paper or cloth, you make a picture of it using paint.
चित्रकारी करना
*He likes **painting** flowers.*
2 If you **paint** a wall or a door, you cover it with paint.
रंगना

painting *noun*
paintings
A **painting** is a picture made with paint.
चित्र
*He's doing a **painting** of a bowl of fruit.*

pair *noun*
pairs
A **pair** of things is two things of the same size and shape that are used together.
जोड़ा
*She wore a **pair** of plain black shoes.*

palace *noun*
palaces
A **palace** is a very large house where important people live.
महल

pale *adjective*
paler, palest
A **pale** colour is not strong or bright.
निष्प्रभ
*She's wearing a **pale** blue dress.*

palm *noun*
palms

1 A **palm** or a **palm tree** is a tree that grows in hot countries. It has long leaves at the top, and no branches.
ताड़ का पेड़

2 The **palm** of your hand is the inside part of your hand, between your fingers and your wrist.
हथेली

panda *noun*
pandas

A **panda** is a large animal with black and white fur.
पांडा

pantomime *noun*
pantomimes

A **pantomime** is a play that has a funny story with music and songs.
मूक अभिनय

paper *noun*
papers

1 **Paper** is a material that you write on or wrap things with.
क़ाग़ज़
*He wrote his name down on a piece of **paper**.*

2 A **paper** is a newspaper.
अख़बार

parcel *noun*
parcels

A **parcel** is something that is wrapped in paper.
पार्सल/पुलिंदा

parent *noun*
parents

Your **parents** are your mother and father.
माता/पिता

park *noun*
parks

A **park** is a place with grass and trees. People go to **parks** to take exercise or play games.
उद्यान

park *verb*
parks, parking, parked

When someone **parks** a car, they leave it somewhere.
निश्चित स्थान पर गाड़ी खड़ी करना
*They **parked** in the street outside the house.*

parrot *noun*
parrots

A **parrot** is a bird with a curved beak and bright feathers.
तोता
Parrots' feet have two toes at the front and two at the back.

part *noun*
parts

Part of something is a piece of it.
हिस्सा

party *noun*
parties

A **party** is a time when people meet to have fun.
दावत
*She's having a birthday **party**.*

pass *verb*
passes, passing, passed

1 When you **pass** someone, you go by them.
पार करना/गुज़रना
*We **passed** them on our way here.*

2 If you **pass** something to someone, you give it to them.
देना
*He **passed** a note to his friend.*

3 If you **pass** a test, you do well.
उत्तीर्ण होना

passenger *noun*
passengers

A **passenger** is a person who is travelling in a vehicle, but who is not driving.
यात्री

A B C D E F G H I J K L M N O P Q R S T U V W X Y Z

past *noun*

The **past** is the period of time before now.
अतीत

*In the **past**, there weren't any computers.*

past

1   Something that is **past** a place is on the other side of it.
के परे
*It's just **past** the school there.*

2   You use **past** when you are telling the time.
अनंतर/के बाद
*It was ten **past** eleven.*

pasta *noun*

Pasta is a mixture of flour, eggs, and water.
पास्ता

Pasta comes in lots of shapes, even letters of the alphabet.

paste *verb*

pastes, pasting, pasted

1   If you **paste** something on to a surface, you stick it with glue.
चिपकाना

2   If you **paste** words or pictures on a computer, you copy them from one place and put them somewhere new.
पेस्ट करना/लगाना (कंप्यूटर के अर्थ में)
*You can **paste** by holding down the Ctrl key and pressing V.*

pastry *noun*

Pastry is a mixture of flour, butter, and water. People make it flat and thin so that they can use it to make pies.
पेस्ट्री

path *noun*

paths

A **path** is a strip of ground that people walk along.
रास्ता

*We followed the **path** along the cliff.*

patient *adjective*

If you are **patient**, you don't get angry quickly.
धैर्यवान

patient *noun*

patients

A **patient** is someone that a nurse or a doctor is looking after.
मरीज़/रोगी

pattern *noun*

patterns

A **pattern** is a group of repeated shapes.
नमूना/आकृति

*The carpet had a **pattern** of light and dark stripes.*

paw *noun*

paws

The **paws** of an animal such as a cat, dog, or bear are its feet.
पंजा

*The kitten was black with white **paws**.*

pay *verb*

pays, paying, paid

If you **pay** for something, you give someone an amount of money for it.
भुगतान करना

*Did you **pay** for those sweets?*

peach *noun*

peaches

A **peach** is a round fruit with a soft red and orange skin.
आड़ू

peanut *noun*

peanuts

Peanuts are small nuts that you can eat.
मूँगफली

pear *noun*

pears

A **pear** is a fruit which is narrow at the top and wide and round at the bottom.
नाशपाती

peas *noun*

Peas are small, round, green vegetables.
मटर

pebble *noun*
pebbles

A **pebble** is a small, smooth stone.
कंकड़

pedal *noun*
pedals

The **pedals** on a bicycle are the two parts that you push with your feet to make the bicycle move.
पेडल

peel *noun*

The **peel** of a fruit is its skin.
छिलका

peg *noun*
pegs

A **peg** is a small piece of metal or wood on a wall that you hang things on.
खूंटी

pen *noun*
pens

A **pen** is a long thin tool that you use for writing with ink.
कलम

pencil *noun*
pencils

A **pencil** is a thin piece of wood with a black material through the middle that you use to write or draw with.
पेंसिल

penguin *noun*
penguins

A **penguin** is a black and white bird that lives in very cold places. **Penguins** can swim but they cannot fly.
पेंग्विन

pentagon *noun*
pentagons

A **pentagon** is a shape with five straight sides.
पंचभुज

people *noun*

People are men, women, and children.
लोग

*Lots of **people** came to the party.*

pepper *noun*
peppers

1   **Pepper** is a powder with a hot taste that you put on food.
काली मिर्च का चूर्ण

2   A **pepper** is a green, red, or yellow vegetable with seeds inside it.
काली मिर्च

period *noun*
periods

A **period** is a length of time.
काल

person *noun*
people

A **person** is a man, a woman, or a child.
व्यक्ति

pest *noun*
pests

Pests are insects or small animals that damage crops or food.
कीट

pet *noun*
pets

A **pet** is a tame animal that you keep in your home.
पालतू

a
b
c
d
e
f
g
h
i
j
k
l
m
n
o
p
q
r
s
t
u
v
w
x
y
z

A
B
C
D
E
F
G
H
I
J
K
L
M
N
O
P
Q
R
S
T
U
V
W
X
Y
Z

petal *noun*
petals

The **petals** of a flower are the thin parts on the outside that are a bright colour.
पंखुड़ी

phone *noun*
phones

A **phone** is a piece of equipment that you use to talk to someone in another place.
फ़ोन
Two minutes later the phone rang.

photograph *noun*
photographs

A **photograph** is a picture that you take with a camera.
छायाचित्र
She took lots of photographs of her friends.

piano *noun*
pianos

A **piano** is a large instrument for playing music. You play it by pressing the black and white keys.
पियानो

pick *verb*
picks, picking, picked

1 If you **pick** someone, you choose them.
   छाँटना/चुनना
2 When you **pick** flowers, fruit, or leaves, you take them from a plant or tree.
   तोड़ना/चुनना
   I've picked some flowers from the garden.

picnic *noun*
picnics

When people have a **picnic**, they eat a meal outside, usually in a park or a forest, or at the beach.
पिकनिक/उद्यान भोज
We're going on a picnic tomorrow.

picture *noun*
pictures

A **picture** is a drawing or painting.
चित्र

pie *noun*
pies

A **pie** is a dish of fruit, meat, or vegetables that is covered with pastry and baked.
समोसे जैसा पकवान
We each had a slice of apple pie.

piece *noun*
pieces

A **piece** of something is a part of it.
टुकड़ा
You must only take one piece of cake.

pig *noun*
pigs

A **pig** is a farm animal with a fat body and short legs.
सूअर

pigeon *noun*
pigeons

A **pigeon** is a large grey bird.
कबूतर

pile *noun*
piles

A **pile** of things is several of them lying on top of each other.
ढेर
We searched through the pile of boxes.

pill *noun*
pills

Pills are small solid round pieces of medicine that you swallow.
गोली

pillow *noun*
pillows

A **pillow** is something soft that you rest your head on when you are in bed.
तकिया

pilot *noun*
pilots

A **pilot** is a person who controls an aircraft.
वायुयान चालक

pin *noun*
pins

A **pin** is a very small thin piece of metal with a point at one end.
पिन

pineapple *noun*
pineapples

A **pineapple** is a large sweet yellow fruit with a lot of juice. Its skin is brown, thick, and very rough.
अन्नानास

pipe *noun*
pipes

A **pipe** is a long tube that water or gas can flow through.
नलिका

*They are going to take out the old water **pipes**.*

pirate *noun*
pirates

Pirates are people who attack ships and steal things from them.
समुद्री लुटेरा

*They have to find the **pirates** and the hidden gold.*

pizza *noun*
pizzas

A **pizza** is a flat, round piece of bread. **Pizzas** are covered with cheese and tomatoes.
पिज़्ज़ा

*Bake the **pizza** in a hot oven.*

place *noun*
places

1 A **place** is a building, area, town, or country.
स्थान
   *This is the **place** where I was born.*

2 A **place** is also where something belongs.
जगह
   *He put the picture back in its **place** on the shelf.*

plain *adjective*
plainer, plainest

Something that is **plain** is ordinary and not special.
सादा

plan *noun*
plans

A **plan** is a way of doing something that you work out before you do it.
योजना

*I've got a **plan** for getting out of here.*

plane *noun*
planes

A **plane** is a large vehicle with wings and engines that flies through the air.
वायुयान

planet *noun*
planets

You find **planets** in space. They move around stars. The Earth is a **planet**.
ग्रह

a
b
c
d
e
f
g
h
i
j
k
l
m
n
o
p
q
r
s
t
u
v
w
x
y
z

A
B
C
D
E
F
G
H
I
J
K
L
M
N
O
P
Q
R
S
T
U
V
W
X
Y
Z

plant *noun*
plants

A **plant** is a living thing that grows in the earth. **Plants** have a stem, leaves, and roots.
पौधा

plaster *noun*
plasters

1 A **plaster** is a strip of material with a soft part in the middle. You can cover a cut on your body with a **plaster**.
चिपकने वाली पट्टी

2 **Plaster** is a paste which people put on walls and ceilings so that they are smooth.
पलस्तर
*There were huge cracks in the **plaster**.*

plastic *noun*

Plastic is a material that is light but strong. It is made in factories.
प्लास्टिक
*He put his sweets in a **plastic** bag.*

plate *noun*
plates

A **plate** is a flat dish that is used for holding food.
तश्तरी
*She pushed her **plate** away.*

platform *noun*
platforms

A **platform** in a station is the place where you wait for a train.
प्लेटफ़ॉर्म

play *verb*
plays, playing, played

1 When you **play**, you spend time using toys and taking part in games.
खेलना
*She was **playing** with her dolls.*

2 If you **play** an instrument, you make music with it.
बजाना

playground *noun*
playgrounds

A **playground** is a special area where children can play.
खेल का मैदान

please

You say **please** when you are asking someone to do something.
कृपया
*Can you help us, **please**?*

plenty *noun*

If there is **plenty** of something, there is a lot of it.
प्रचुरता
*Don't worry. There's still **plenty** of time.*

plough *noun*
ploughs

A **plough** is a large tool that is used on a farm. Farmers pull it across a field to make the earth loose, so that they can plant seeds.
हल

plus

You say **plus** to show that you are adding one number to another.
और/जोड़
*Two **plus** two is four.*

pocket *noun*
pockets

A **pocket** is a small bag that is part of your clothes.
जेब
*He put the key in his **pocket**.*

poem *noun*
poems

A **poem** is a piece of writing. When people write a **poem**, they choose the words in a very careful way, so that they sound beautiful.
कविता

point *noun*
points

1 The **point** of something is its thin, sharp end. Needles and knives have **points**.
नोक

2 A **point** is a mark that you win in a game or a sport.
अंक

point *verb*
points, pointing, pointed

If you **point** at something, you stick out your finger to show where it is.
इंगित करना
*I **pointed** at the boy sitting near me.*

poisonous *adjective*

Something that is **poisonous** will kill you or hurt you if you swallow or touch it.
ज़हरीला

polar bear *noun*
polar bears

A **polar bear** is a large white bear which lives in the area around the North Pole.
ध्रुवीय भालू

police

The **police** are the people who make sure that people obey the law.
पुलिस

polite *adjective*

Someone who is **polite** behaves well.
नम्र

pond *noun*
ponds

A **pond** is a small area of water.
तालाब
*We can feed the ducks on the **pond**.*

pony *noun*
ponies

A **pony** is a small horse.
टट्टू

poor *adjective*
poorer, poorest

Someone who is **poor** doesn't have much money and doesn't own many things.
गरीब

possible *adjective*

If something is **possible** it can happen.
संभव

post *verb*
posts, posting, posted

If you **post** a letter, you put a stamp on it and send it to someone.
डाक में डालना

poster *noun*
posters

A **poster** is a large notice or picture that you stick on a wall.
इश्तिहार/पोस्टर

potato *noun*
potatoes

Potatoes are hard round white vegetables with brown or red skins. They grow under the ground.
आलू

a b c d e f g h i j k l m n o p q r s t u v w x y z

A B C D E F G H I J K L M N O P Q R S T U V W X Y Z

pour *verb*
pours, pouring, poured
If you **pour** something like water, you make it flow out of a container.
ढालना

powder *noun*
Powder is a fine dry dust, like flour.
चूर्ण

power *noun*
1 If someone has **power**, they have control over people.
शक्ति/अधिकार
*He has the **power** to keep you in after school.*

2 The **power** of something is its strength.
शक्ति/ताक़त
*The engine doesn't often work at full **power**.*

practise *verb*
practises, practising, practised
If you **practise** something, you do it often in order to do it better.
अभ्यास करना
*I've been **practising** my song.*

present *noun*
presents
1 The **present** is the period of time that is taking place now.
वर्तमान

2 A **present** is something that you give to someone for them to keep.
उपहार
*She got a **present** for her birthday.*

present *adjective*
If someone is **present** somewhere, they are there.
मौजूद/उपस्थित होना
*He wasn't **present** when they called out his name.*

press *verb*
presses, pressing, pressed
If you **press** something, you push it hard.
दबाना
***Press** the blue button.*

pretend *verb*
pretends, pretending, pretended
When you **pretend**, you act as if something is true, when you know it isn't.
ढोंग करना
*She **pretended** to be the teacher.*

pretty *adjective*
prettier, prettiest
If something is **pretty**, it is nice to look at.
सुंदर
*She was wearing a **pretty** necklace.*

price *noun*
prices
The **price** of something is how much you have to pay to buy it.
कीमत
*Could you tell me the **price** of this car, please?*

prick *verb*
pricks, pricking, pricked
If you **prick** something, you stick something sharp like a pin or a knife into it.
चुभाना
*She **pricked** her finger on a pin.*

prince *noun*
princes
A **prince** is a boy or a man in the family of a king or queen.
राजकुमार

princess *noun*
princesses
A **princess** is a girl or a woman in the family of a king or queen.
राजकुमारी

print *verb*
prints, printing, printed

1 If you **print** something, you use a machine to put words or pictures on paper.
छापना/मुद्रित करना

2 If you **print** when you are writing, you do not join the letters together.
छापना/मुद्रित करना

prison *noun*
prisons

A **prison** is a building where people who have broken the law are kept as a punishment.
कारावास/जेल

*He was sent to **prison** for five years.*

prize *noun*
prizes

A **prize** is money or a special thing that you give to the person who wins a game, a race, or a competition.
पुरस्कार

*He won first **prize**.*

problem *noun*
problems

A **problem** is something or someone that makes thing difficult, or that makes you worry.
समस्या

program *noun*
programs

A **program** is a set of instructions that a computer uses to do a job.
प्रोग्राम - कंप्यूटर संबंधी निर्देश

programme *noun*
programmes

A **programme** is a television or radio show.
कार्यक्रम

*She is watching her favourite television **programme**.*

project *noun*
projects

A **project** is a plan that takes a lot of time and effort.
परियोजना

*It was a large building **project**.*

promise *verb*
promises, promising, promised

If you **promise** to do something, you say that you will be sure to do it.
वादा करना

*I **promise** that I'll help you all I can.*

pronoun *noun*
pronouns

A **pronoun** is a word that you use in place of a noun when you are talking about someone or something. "It" and "she" are **pronouns**.
सर्वनाम

proper *adjective*

The **proper** thing or way is the one that is right.
यथोचित

*Put things in their **proper** place.*

protect *verb*
protects, protecting, protected

If you **protect** something, you keep it safe.
रक्षा करना

*Make sure you **protect** your skin from the sun.*

proud *adjective*
prouder, proudest

If you feel **proud**, you feel pleased about something good that you or other people close to you have done.
गर्वित

*I was **proud** of our team today.*

pudding *noun*
puddings

A **pudding** is something sweet that you eat after your main meal.
खाने के बाद परोसा जाने वाला मिष्ठान

*We had a delicious chocolate **pudding**.*

a b c d e f g h i j k l m n o p q r s t u v w x y z

A
B
C
D
E
F
G
H
I
J
K
L
M
N
O
P
Q
R
S
T
U
V
W
X
Y
Z

puddle *noun*
puddles

A **puddle** is a small amount of water on the ground.
गड़ही
*Splashing in **puddles** is lots of fun.*

pull *verb*
pulls, pulling, pulled

When you **pull** something, you hold it and move it towards you.
खींचना
*The dentist had to **pull** out all his teeth.*

punishment *noun*
punishments

Punishment is something done to someone because they have done something wrong.
सज़ा
*His father sent him to bed early as a **punishment** for being rude.*

pupil *noun*
pupils

The **pupils** at a school are the children who go there.
शिष्य/विद्यार्थी
*Around 200 **pupils** go to this school.*

puppet *noun*
puppets

A **puppet** is a small model of a person or animal that you can move.
कठपुतली

puppy *noun*
puppies

A **puppy** is a young dog.
पिल्ला

purple *noun*

Purple is a mixture of red and blue.
बैंगनी
*Some grapes are **purple**.*

purse *noun*
purses

A **purse** is a small bag that women use to carry money and other things.
बटुआ
*She reached in her **purse** for her money.*

push *verb*
pushes, pushing, pushed

When you **push** something, you press it in order to move it away from you.
धक्का देना
*I **pushed** back my chair and stood up.*

put *verb*
puts, putting, put

When you **put** something somewhere, you move it there.
रखना
*He **put** the book on the desk.*

puzzle *verb*
puzzles, puzzling, puzzled

If something **puzzles** you, you do not understand it and you feel confused.
उलझन में डालना
*There was something about her that **puzzled** me.*

pyjamas *noun*

Pyjamas are loose trousers and a jacket that you wear in bed.
पैजामा

pyramid *noun*
pyramids

A **pyramid** is a solid shape with a flat base and flat sides that make a point where they meet at the top.
पिरामिड

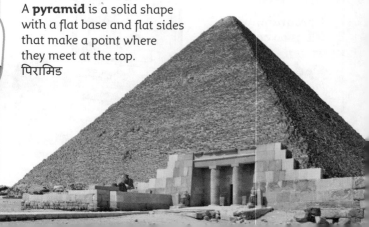

quack *verb*
quacks, quacking, quacked

When a duck **quacks**,
it makes a loud sound.
बत्तख की बोली
There were ducks
quacking *on the lawn.*

quarrel *noun*
quarrels

A **quarrel** is an angry argument between people.
झगड़ा
I had an awful ***quarrel*** *with my brothers.*

quarter *noun*
quarters

A **quarter** is one of four equal parts of something.
चौथाई
My sister ate a ***quarter*** *of the chocolate cake.*

queen *noun*
queens

A **queen** is a woman
who rules a country,
or a woman who is
married to a king.
रानी
The crowd cheered when
the ***queen*** *went past.*

question *noun*
questions

A **question** is something that you say or write to ask a
person about something.
प्रश्न
They asked her a lot of ***questions*** *about her holiday.*

queue *noun*
queues

A **queue** is a line of people or cars waiting
for something.
कतार/पंक्ति
He stood in the lunch ***queue***
for ten minutes.

quick *adjective*
quicker, quickest

Something that is **quick** moves or does things with
great speed.
फुर्तीला
The cat was so ***quick*** *that I couldn't catch it.*

quickly

If you move or do something **quickly** you do it with
great speed.
शीघ्रता से
The girl ran ***quickly*** *along the street.*

quiet *adjective*
quieter, quietest

Someone who is **quiet** makes only a small amount of
noise or no noise at all.
शांत
The baby was so ***quiet*** *I didn't know he was there.*

quite

Quite means a bit but not a lot.
अत्यंत
I ***quite*** *like her but she's not my best friend.*

quiz *noun*
quizzes

A **quiz** is a game in which someone asks you
questions to find out what you know.
प्रश्नोत्तरी
After dinner we had a TV ***quiz*** *and our team won.*

a b c d e f g h i j k l m n o p q r s t u v w x y z

A B C D E F G H I J K L M N O P Q R S T U V W X Y Z

rabbit noun
rabbits

A **rabbit** is a small animal with long ears. **Rabbits** live in holes in the ground.
खरगोश
The children were excited when they heard they were getting a pet rabbit.

race noun
races

A **race** is a competition to see who is fastest, for example in running or driving.
दौड़/दौड़ प्रतियोगिता
Nobody can beat my sister in a race.

radiator noun
radiators

A **radiator** is a metal thing filled with hot water or steam. **Radiators** keep rooms warm.
विकिरक
I burned myself on the radiator in the bathroom.

radio noun
radios

A **radio** is a piece of equipment you use to hear programmes with talking, news and music.
रेडियो
Turn on the radio for the news please.

railway noun
railways

A **railway** is a special road for trains, with stations along it. **Railways** have two metal lines that are always the same distance apart.
रेल मार्ग
The house was beside the railway.

rain noun

Rain is water that falls from the clouds in small drops.
वर्षा
My mother told me not to go out in the rain.

rainbow noun
rainbows

A **rainbow** is a half circle of different colours in the sky. You can sometimes see a **rainbow** when it rains.
इंद्रधनुष
A rainbow appeared when the storm was over.

ran

⇨ Look at **run**.
I ran to school because I was late.

rang

⇨ Look at **ring**.
I got worried when the phone rang.

rare adjective
rarer, rarest

Something that is **rare** is not seen or heard very often.
दुर्लभ
We are lucky to see this bird because it is very rare.

raspberry noun
raspberries

A **raspberry** is a small soft red fruit. **Raspberries** grow on bushes.
रसभरी
Would you like some raspberries with your ice cream?

rat noun
rats

A **rat** is an animal that looks like a mouse. A **rat** has a long tail and sharp teeth.
चूहा
The old house was full of rats.

rather

You use **rather** to mean "a little bit".
कुछ हद तक
I thought the party was rather boring.

raw *adjective*

Raw food has not been cooked.
कच्चा
*There is a bowl of **raw** carrots and cauliflower on the table.*

reach *verb*
reaches, reaching, reached

1 When you **reach** a place, you arrive there.
पहुँचना
*We will not **reach** home until midnight.*

2 If you **reach** somewhere, you move your arm and hand to take or touch something.
हाथ बढ़ाना
*I **reached** into my bag and brought out a pen.*

read *verb*
reads, reading, read

When you **read**, you look at written words and understand them, and sometimes say them aloud.
पढ़ना
*My father **reads** me a story every night before I go to sleep.*

ready *adjective*

If you are **ready**, you are able to do something or go somewhere right now.
तैयार
*It takes her a long time to get **ready** for school.*

real *adjective*

1 Something that is **real** is true and is not imagined.
वास्तविक
*No, it wasn't a dream. It was **real**.*

2 If something is **real**, it is not a copy.
असली
*Is your necklace **real** gold?*

really

1 You say **really** to show how much you mean something.
सचमुच
*I'm **really** sorry I can't come to your party.*

2 You say **really** to show that what you are saying is true.
वास्तव में
*Are we **really** going to the zoo?*

reason *noun*
reasons

The **reason** for something is the fact which explains why it happens.
कारण
*You must have a good **reason** for being so late.*

receive *verb*
receives, receiving, received

When you **receive** something, someone gives it to you, or you get it after it has been sent to you.
प्राप्त करना
*Did you **receive** the birthday card I sent you?*

recipe *noun*
recipes

A **recipe** is a list of food and a set of instructions telling you how to cook something.
व्यंजन विधि
*Do you have a **recipe** for chocolate cake?*

recite *verb*
recites, reciting, recited

When someone **recites** a poem or other piece of writing, they say it aloud after they have learned it.
सुनाना
*We each had to **recite** a poem in front of the class.*

record *noun*
records

A **record** is the best result ever.
कीर्तिमान
*What's the world **record** for the 100 metres?*

record *verb*
records, recording, recorded

If you **record** something like a TV programme, you make a copy of it so that you can watch it later.
रिकॉर्ड करना
*Can you **record** the football for me please?*

recorder *noun*
recorders

A **recorder** is a small instrument in the shape of a pipe. You play a **recorder** by blowing into it and putting your fingers over the holes in it.
बाँसुरी जैसा वाद्ययंत्र
*He has been learning the **recorder** for three years.*

a
b
c
d
e
f
g
h
i
j
k
l
m
n
o
p
q
r
s
t
u
v
w
x
y
z

A B C D E F G H I J K L M N O P Q **R** S T U V W X Y Z

rectangle *noun*
rectangles

A **rectangle** is a shape with four straight sides.
आयत

red *noun*

Red is the colour of blood or a strawberry.
लाल
*Her dress is bright **red**.*

reflection *noun*
reflections

A **reflection** is something you can see on a smooth, shiny surface. What you see is really in a different place.
प्रतिबिंब

***Reflections** always show things the wrong way round.*

refuse *verb*
refuses, refusing, refused

If you **refuse** to do something, you say that you will not do it.
मना करना
*He **refuses** to have a bath.*

remember *verb*
remembers, remembering, remembered

If you **remember** people or things from the past, you can bring them into your mind and think about them.
याद रखना
*I **remember** the first time I met him.*

remind *verb*
reminds, reminding, reminded

If someone **reminds** you about something, they help you to remember it.
याद दिलाना
***Remind** me to buy a bottle of milk, will you?*

remove *verb*
removes, removing, removed

If you **remove** something from a place, you take it away.
हटाना
*When the cake is cooked, **remove** it from the oven.*

repair *verb*
repairs, repairing, repaired

If you **repair** something that is damaged or broken, you fix it so that it works again.
मरम्मत करना
*The man managed to **repair** the broken tap.*

repeat *verb*
repeats, repeating, repeated

If you **repeat** something, you say it, write it, or do it again.
दोहराना
*Please can you **repeat** the question?*

reply *verb*
replies, replying, replied

If you **reply** to something, you say or write an answer.
जवाब देना
*Will you please **reply** when I ask you a question.*

reptile *noun*
reptiles

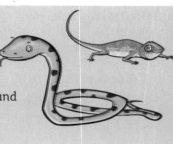

A **reptile** is an animal that has cold blood, rough skin, and lays eggs. Snakes and lizards are **reptiles**.
सरीसृप

rescue *verb*
rescues, rescuing, rescued

If you **rescue** someone, you help them get away from a dangerous place.
बचाना/छुड़ाना
*The police **rescued** 20 people from the roof of the building.*

rest *verb*
rests, resting, rested

If you **rest**, you sit or lie down and do not do anything active for a while.
आराम करना
*My grandmother always **rests** in the afternoon.*

rest *noun*

The **rest** is the parts of something that are left.
शेष भाग
*Who ate the **rest** of the cake?*

restaurant *noun*
restaurants

A **restaurant** is a place where you can buy and eat a meal.
रेस्तराँ/भोजनालय
*We had lunch in an Italian **restaurant**.*

result *noun*
results

A **result** is something that happens because another thing has happened.
परिणाम
*I got measles and as a **result** was off school for two weeks.*

return *verb*
returns, returning, returned

1   When you **return** to a place, you go back to it after you have been away.
वापस लौटना
*He **returned** to Japan after his holiday in England.*

2   If you **return** something to someone, you give it back to them.
वापस करना/लौटाना
*I forgot to **return** my library books.*

reward *noun*
rewards

A **reward** is something that is given to a person because they have done something good.
ईनाम
*The school gives **rewards** to children who behave well.*

rhinoceros *noun*
rhinoceroses

A **rhinoceros** is a large wild animal with thick grey skin. A **rhinoceros** has one or two horns on its nose.
गैंडा

rhyme *verb*
rhymes, rhyming, rhymed

If two words **rhyme**, they have the same sound at the end of them.
तुकबंदी होना
*Sally **rhymes** with valley.*

rhythm *noun*
rhythms

Rhythm is something which is repeated again and again in the same way.
ताल
*Listen to the **rhythm** of the music.*

rib *noun*
ribs

Your **ribs** are the 12 pairs of curved bones that go round your body.
पसली
*He fell off his bike and broke a **rib**.*

ribbon *noun*
ribbons

A **ribbon** is a long narrow piece of cloth. You use **ribbons** to decorate things or tie them together.
फीता
*The girl's hair was tied with a blue and white **ribbon**.*

rice *noun*

Rice is white or brown grains from a plant. **Rice** grows in wet areas.
चावल
*The meal was chicken, **rice**, and vegetables.*

rich *adjective*
richer, richest

Someone who is **rich** has a lot of money and expensive things.
धनवान
*She is a **rich** woman who owns a very large house.*

riddle *noun*
riddles

A **riddle** is a question that seems to be nonsense, but that has a clever answer.
पहेली
*He asked the **riddle**, "What key cannot open a door?" and I answered, "a monkey".*

a
b
c
d
e
f
g
h
i
j
k
l
m
n
o
p
q
r
s
t
u
v
w
x
y
z

A
B
C
D
E
F
G
H
I
J
K
L
M
N
O
P
Q
R
S
T
U
V
W
X
Y
Z

ride verb
rides, riding, rode, ridden

When you **ride** a horse or a bike, you sit on it and control it as it moves along.
सवारी करना
*The girl **rode** her horse along the beach.*

right adjective

1 If something is **right**, it is correct and there have been no mistakes.
सही
*Only one child in the class knew the **right** answer to the teacher's question.*

2 The **right** side is the side that is towards the east when you look north.
दायां
*Most people write with their **right** hand.*

ring verb
rings, ringing, rang, rung

When a bell **rings**, it makes a clear, loud sound.
घंटी बजना
*The school bell **rings** at nine o'clock.*

ring noun
rings

A **ring** is a round piece of metal that you wear on a finger.
अँगूठी
*He turned the **ring** on his finger.*

ripe adjective
riper, ripest

When fruit or grain is **ripe**, it is ready to be eaten.
पका हुआ
*Don't eat the apples until they are **ripe**.*

rise verb
rises, rising, rose, risen

If something **rises**, it moves up.
उठना
*We watched the balloon **rise** into the sky.*

river noun
rivers

A **river** is a long line of water that flows into the sea.
नदी
*The Nile is one of the longest **rivers** in the world.*

road noun
roads

A **road** is a long piece of hard ground for vehicles to travel on.
सड़क
*You must look both ways before you cross the **road**.*

roar verb
roars, roaring, roared

If a person, an animal or a thing **roars**, they make a very loud noise.
गरजना
*The engines **roared** and the aeroplane started to move.*

robot noun
robots

A **robot** is a machine that can move and do things that it has been told to do.
यंत्रमानव
*We have **robots** that we could send to the moon.*

rock noun
rocks

1 **Rock** is the hard material that is in the ground and in mountains.
चट्टान
*We tried to dig, but the ground was solid **rock**.*

2 A **rock** is a piece of this material.
शिला/चट्टान
*She picked up a **rock** and threw it into the lake.*

rock verb
rocks, rocking, rocked

If something **rocks**, it moves from side to side.
डोलना

rocket noun
rockets

A **rocket** is a vehicle that people use to travel into space.
रॉकेट
*This is the **rocket** that took them to the moon.*

rode
⇨ Look at **ride**.
*The man **rode** his bike down the hill.*

roll *verb*
rolls, rolling, rolled

When something **rolls**, it moves along a surface, turning over and over.
लुढ़कना
*The ball bounced out of the garden and **rolled** across the road.*

roof *noun*
roofs

The **roof** of a building is the bit on top that covers it.
छत
*Our house is the one with the red **roof**.*

room *noun*
rooms

1 A **room** is a part of a building that has its own walls.
कमरा
*A minute later he left the **room**.*

2 If there is **room** somewhere, there is a enough empty space.
जगह
*There isn't **room** for any more furniture in here.*

root *noun*
roots

The **roots** of a plant are the parts of it that grow under the ground.
जड़
*She dug a hole near the **roots** of an apple tree.*

rope *noun*
ropes

A **rope** is a type of very thick string that is made by twisting together several strings or wires.
रस्सी
*He tied the **rope** around his waist.*

rose *noun*
roses

A **rose** is a large garden flower with a lovely smell. **Roses** grow on bushes.
गुलाब
*The teacher was given a bunch of red **roses**.*

rough *adjective*
rougher, roughest

1 If something is **rough**, it is not smooth or even.
खुरदुरा/ऊबड़खाबड़
*His hands were **rough**.*

2 If you are **rough**, you are not being careful or gentle.
रूखा/कड़ा
*Don't be so **rough** or you'll break it.*

round *adjective*
rounder, roundest

Something **round** is in the shape of a ball or a circle.
गोलाकार
*There was a **round** table in the middle of the room.*

row *noun*
rows

A **row** is a line of things or people.
पंक्ति
*Our house is opposite a **row** of shops.*

rub *verb*
rubs, rubbing, rubbed

If you **rub** something, you move your hand or a cloth backwards and forwards over it.
रगड़ना
*I **rubbed** the window and looked outside.*

rubber *noun*
rubbers

1 **Rubber** is a strong material that stretches. **Rubber** is used to make things like tyres and boots for wet weather.
रबड़

2 A **rubber** is a small piece of rubber used to remove pencil mistakes.
रबड़
*Have you got a **rubber** in your pencil case?*

a b c d e f g h i j k l m n o p q **r** s t u v w x y z

A
B
C
D
E
F
G
H
I
J
K
L
M
N
O
P
Q
R
S
T
U
V
W
X
Y
Z

rubbish *noun*

Rubbish is things like empty packs and used paper that you throw away.
बकवास/बेकार

rude *adjective*
ruder, rudest

If people are **rude**, they are not polite.
अशिष्ट
*It is **rude** to ask for something without saying "please".*

ruin *verb*
ruins, ruining, ruined

If you **ruin** something, you destroy or spoil it.
बर्बाद करना/बिगाड़ना
*The rain **ruined** the party.*

rule *noun*
rules

Rules are instructions that tell you what you must do or must not do.
नियम
*Can you explain the **rules** of cricket to me?*

rule *verb*
rules, ruling, ruled

Someone who **rules** a country controls it.
शासन करना

ruler *noun*
rulers

1 A **ruler** is a long, flat piece of wood or plastic with straight edges. You use a **ruler** for measuring things or drawing straight lines.
पैमाना

2 A **ruler** is also a person who rules a country.
शासक
*He was **ruler** of France at that time.*

run *verb*
runs, running, ran, run

When you **run**, you move very quickly on your legs.
दौड़ना
*It's very dangerous to **run** across the road.*

rung

⇨ Look at **ring**.
*They had **rung** the door bell when I was in the shower.*

sad *adjective*
sadder, saddest

If you are **sad**, you don't feel happy.
दुःखी
*I'm **sad** that he is leaving.*

safe *adjective*
safer, safest

If you are **safe**, you are not in any danger.
सुरक्षित
*Is it **safe**?*

said

⇨ Look at **say**.
*That is what she **said** to me.*

sail *noun*
sails

Sails are large pieces of cloth on a boat that catch the wind and move the boat along.
पाल/मस्तूल

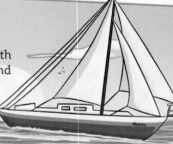

salad *noun*
salads

A **salad** is a mixture of vegetables and sometimes other foods. You usually eat **salads** cold.
सलाद

salt *noun*

Salt is a white powder that you use to make food taste better.
नमक
*Now add **salt** and pepper.*

same *adjective*

If two things are the **same**, they are like one another.
एक जैसा
*The two cats look the **same**.*

sand *noun*

Sand is a powder made of very small pieces of stone. Deserts and most beaches are made of **sand**.
रेत

sandal *noun*
sandals

Sandals are light shoes that you wear in warm weather.
सैंडल
*He put on a pair of old **sandals**.*

sandwich *noun*
sandwiches

A **sandwich** is two slices of bread with another food such as cheese or meat between them.
सैंडविच
*She ate a large **sandwich**.*

sang

⇨ Look at **sing**.
*She **sang** a happy song.*

sank

⇨ Look at **sink**.
*The boat **sank** in the storm.*

sari *noun*
saris

A **sari** is a long piece of material worn folded around the body by women.
साड़ी
*She was wearing a new yellow **sari**.*

sat

⇨ Look at **sit**.
*She **sat** down next to the fire.*

satellite *noun*
satellites

A **satellite** is a machine that is sent into space to receive and send back information.
उपग्रह

Saturday *noun*
Saturdays

Saturday is the day after Friday and before Sunday.
शनिवार
*He called her on **Saturday** morning.*

saucepan *noun*
saucepans

A **saucepan** is a deep metal container with a long handle and a lid. **Saucepans** are used for cooking.
पकाने का हत्थेदार बर्तन
*Put the potatoes in a **saucepan** and boil them.*

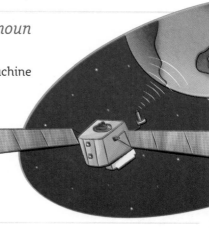

saucer *noun*
saucers

A **saucer** is a small curved plate that you put under a cup.
तश्तरी

a
b
c
d
e
f
g
h
i
j
k
l
m
n
o
p
q
r
s
t
u
v
w
x
y
z

A
B
C
D
E
F
G
H
I
J
K
L
M
N
O
P
Q
R
S
T
U
V
W
X
Y
Z

sausage *noun*
sausages

A **sausage** is a mixture of very small pieces of meat and other foods, inside a long thin skin.
सॉसेज - मांस से भरी खाद्यवस्तु

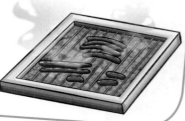

save *verb*
saves, saving, saved

1 If you **save** someone or something, you help them to escape from danger.
बचाना
*He **saved** the boy from drowning.*

2 If you **save** something, you keep it because you will need it later.
बचाकर रखना
*She was **saving** her money.*

saw

⇨ Look at **see**.
*We **saw** her walking down the street.*

saw *noun*
saws

A **saw** is a metal tool for cutting wood.
आरी
*He used a **saw** to cut the branches off the tree.*

say *verb*
says, saying, said

When you **say** something, you talk.
कहना
*She **said** that they were very pleased.*

scale *noun*
scales

Scales are small, flat pieces of hard skin that cover the body of animals like fish and snakes.
परत

scales *noun*

Scales are a machine used for weighing things.
तराजू
*He weighed flour on the **scales**.*

scared *adjective*

If you are **scared** of something it frightens you.
भयभीत
*She is **scared** of spiders.*

school *noun*
schools

A **school** is a place where people go to learn.
विद्यालय
*The **school** was built in the 1960s.*

science *noun*
sciences

Science is the study of natural things.
विज्ञान

scissors *noun*

Scissors are a small tool for cutting with two sharp parts that are joined together.
कैंची
*Cut the card using **scissors**.*

score *verb*
scores, scoring, scored

If you **score** in a game, you get a goal, run, or point.
अंक प्राप्त करना
*He **scored** his second goal of the game.*

scratch *verb*
scratches, scratching, scratched

1 If a sharp thing **scratches** someone or something, it makes small cuts on their skin or on its surface.
खरोंचना
*The branches **scratched** my face.*

2 If you **scratch** part of your body, you rub your nails against your skin.
खुजाना/खरोंचना
*He **scratched** his head.*

scream *verb*
screams, screaming, screamed

If you **scream**, you shout or cry in a loud, high voice.
चीखना
*She **screamed** when she saw the spider.*

screen noun
screens
A **screen** is a flat surface on which a picture is shown.
चित्रपट/परदा
*There was dust on the television **screen**.*

sea noun
seas
A **sea** is a large area of salt water.
समुद्र
*They swam in the warm **sea**.*

seal verb
seals, sealing, sealed
When you **seal** an envelope, you close it by folding part of it and sticking it down.
मुहरबंद करना/बंद करना
*He **sealed** the envelope and put on a stamp.*

search verb
searches, searching, searched
If you **search** for something or someone, you look for them everywhere.
खोज
*I am **searching** for my glasses.*

seaside noun
The **seaside** is an area next to the sea.
समुद्रतटीय क्षेत्र
*I went to spend a few days at the **seaside**.*

season noun
seasons
The **seasons** are the four parts of a year: spring, summer, autumn and winter.
मौसम
*Spring is my favourite **season**.*

seat noun
seats
A **seat** is something that you can sit on.
सीट/आसन

second adjective
The **second** thing in a number of things is the one that you count as number two.
दूसरा
*It was the **second** day of his holiday.*

second noun
seconds
A **second** is an amount of time. There are sixty **seconds** in one minute.
सेकेंड/पल
*For a few **seconds** nobody spoke.*

secret adjective
If something is **secret**, only a small number of people know about it, and they do not tell any other people.
गोपनीय/गुप्त
*He knew a **secret** place to hide in the garden.*

see verb
sees, seeing, saw, seen
1 If you **see** something, you are looking at it or you notice it.
देखना
*The fog was so thick we couldn't **see** anything.*

2 If you **see** someone, you meet them.
भेंट करना
*I **saw** him yesterday.*

seed noun
seeds
A **seed** is the small, hard part of a plant from which a new plant grows.
बीज
*Plant the **seeds** in the garden.*

seem verb
seems, seeming, seemed
If something **seems** to be true, it appears to be true or you think it is true.
प्रतीत होना
*The thunder **seemed** very close.*

a
b
c
d
e
f
g
h
i
j
k
l
m
n
o
p
q
r
s
t
u
v
w
x
y
z

seen

⇨ Look at **see**.
*She had **seen** the film before.*

sell *verb*
sells, selling, sold

If you **sell** something, you let someone have it in return for money.
बेचना
*The man **sold** his bike.*

semicircle *noun*
semicircles

A **semicircle** is a half of a circle, or something with this shape.
अर्धवृत्त
*The children stood in a **semicircle**.*

send *verb*
sends, sending, sent

When you **send** someone a message or a parcel, you make it go to them.
भेजना
*I will **send** you a letter when I arrive.*

sensible *adjective*

If you do something **sensible**, you have thought about it a lot first.
समझदार
*The **sensible** thing is not to touch it.*

sent

⇨ Look at **send**.
*He **sent** a letter home.*

September *noun*

September is the month after August and before October. It has 30 days.
सितंबर

serve *verb*
serves, serving, served

Someone who **serves** customers in a shop or a restaurant helps them with what they want to buy.
सेवा करना/ परोसना
*She **served** me coffee and pie.*

set *noun*
sets

A **set** of things is a number of things that belong together.
समुच्चय
*I'll need a **set** of clean clothes.*

seven

Seven is the number **7**.
सात

several *adjective*

You use **several** for talking about a number of people or things that is not large but is greater than two.
कई
*There were **several** boxes on the table.*

sew *verb*
sews, sewing, sewed, sewn

When you **sew** pieces of cloth together, you join them using a needle and thread.
सीना/सिलाई करना
*I must **sew** a button on to this shirt.*

sex *noun*
sexes

The **sex** of a person or animal is if it is male or female.
लिंग
*What **sex** is the baby?*

shadow *noun*
shadows

A **shadow** is a dark shape on a surface that is made when something blocks the light.
परछाई
*The **shadows** of the trees crossed their path.*

shake *verb*
shakes, shaking, shook, shaken

1   If you **shake** something, you hold it and move it quickly up and down.
हिलाना
***Shake** the bottle before you drink.*

2   If someone or something **shakes**, they move quickly backwards and forwards or up and down.
हिलना
*My body was **shaking** with cold.*

shallow *adjective*
shallower, shallowest

If something is **shallow**, it is not deep.
छिछला
*The river is very **shallow** here.*

shape *noun*
shapes

The **shape** of something is the way its outside edges or surfaces look.
आकार
*Pasta comes in different **shapes** and sizes.*

share *verb*
shares, sharing, shared

If you **share** something with another person, you both have it or use it.
साझा करना
*We **shared** an ice cream.*

shark *noun*
sharks

A **shark** is a very large fish. **Sharks** have very sharp teeth and some may attack people.
शार्क

sharp *adjective*
sharper, sharpest

1   A **sharp** point or edge is very thin and can cut through things quickly.
धारदार/पैना
*Be careful, the scissors are **sharp**.*

2   A **sharp** feeling is sudden and is very big or strong.
तीव्र
*I felt a **sharp** pain in my right leg.*

shave *verb*
shaves, shaving, shaved

If you **shave**, you remove hair from your face or body by cutting it off.
हजामत करना
*Rahim took a bath and **shaved**.*

shed *noun*
sheds

A **shed** is a small building where you store things.
छप्पर
*The house has a large **shed** in the garden.*

she'd

1   **She'd** is short for **she had**.
उसने कर लिया है
***She'd** already seen them.*

2   **She'd** is also short for **she would**.
वह करेगी'
***She'd** be very happy.*

sheep *noun*
sheep

A **sheep** is a farm animal with thick hair called wool. Farmers keep **sheep** for their wool or for their meat.
भेड़

sheet *noun*
sheets

1   A **sheet** is a large piece of cloth that you sleep on or cover yourself with in bed.
चादर
*Once a week, we change the **sheets**.*

2   A **sheet** is a piece of paper, glass, plastic, or metal.
पत्तर/चद्दर
*He folded the **sheets** of paper.*

a
b
c
d
e
f
g
h
i
j
k
l
m
n
o
p
q
r
s
t
u
v
w
x
y
z

shelf *noun*
shelves

A **shelf** is a long flat piece of wood on a wall or in a cupboard that you can keep things on.
ताखा
*Dad took a book from the **shelf**.*

shell *noun*
shells

1 The **shell** of an egg or nut is its hard part.
कवच/कड़ा छिलका

2 The **shell** of an animal such as a snail is the hard part that covers its back and protects it.
कवच/आवरण

she'll

She'll is short for **she will**.
वह करेगी
***She'll** be back.*

she's

She's is short for **she is**.
वह है
***She's** a doctor.*

shine *verb*
shines, shining, shone

If something **shines**, it gives out bright light.
चमकना
*Today it's warm and the sun is **shining**.*

shiny *adjective*
shinier, shiniest

If something is **shiny**, it is bright.
चमकीला
*Her hair was **shiny** and clean.*

ship *noun*
ships

A **ship** is a large boat that carries people or things.
जहाज़
*The **ship** was ready to leave.*

shirt *noun*
shirts

A **shirt** is something you wear on the top part of your body. It has a collar and buttons.
कमीज

shiver *verb*
shivers, shivering, shivered

If you **shiver**, your body shakes because you are cold or scared.
काँपना
*She **shivered** with cold.*

shoe *noun*
shoes

Shoes are a type of clothing that you wear on your feet.
जूता
*I need a new pair of **shoes**.*

shone

⇨ Look at **shine**.
*The sun **shone** all day.*

shop *noun*
shops

A **shop** is a place that sells things.
दुकान
*He and his wife run a clothes **shop**.*

shore *noun*
shores

The **shore** of a sea or lake is the land along the edge of it.
किनारा
*They walked slowly down to the **shore**.*

short *adjective*
shorter, shortest

1 If something is **short**, it does not last very long.
छोटा/संक्षिप्त
*Last year we all went to the seaside for a **short** holiday.*

2 A **short** thing is small in length, distance, or height.
छोटा/ नाटा
*She has **short**, straight hair.*

A B C D E F G H I J K L M N O P Q R S T U V W X Y Z

shorts *noun*

Shorts are trousers with short legs.
घुटने तक की पतलून

*He was wearing blue **shorts**.*

should *verb*

You use **should** when you are saying what is the right thing to do.
चाहिए

*He **should** tell us what happened.*

shoulder *noun*
shoulders

Your **shoulders** are the two parts of your body between your neck and the tops of your arms.
कंधा

*Put your hands on the **shoulders** of the person in front of you.*

shout *verb*
shouts, shouting, shouted

If you **shout**, you say something in a very loud voice.
चिल्लाना

*He **shouted** something to his brother.*

show *verb*
shows, showing, showed, shown

1   If you **show** someone something, you let them see it.
दिखाना

*She **showed** me her ring.*

2   If you **show** someone how to do something, you teach them how to do it.
दर्शाना/समझाना

*She **showed** us how to make pasta.*

shower *noun*
showers

1   A **shower** is a thing that you stand under, that covers you with water so you can wash yourself.
फुहारा

*I was in the **shower** when the phone rang.*

2   A **shower** is a short period of rain.
बौछार

*A few **showers** are expected tomorrow.*

shown

⇨ Look at **show**.

*I've **shown** them how to do it.*

shut *verb*
shuts, shutting, shut

If you **shut** something, you close it.
बंद करना

*Please **shut** the gate.*

shy *adjective*
shyer, shyest

If you are **shy**, you are nervous about talking to people that you do not know well.
शर्मीला

*She was a **shy**, quiet girl.*

sick *adjective*
sicker, sickest

If you are **sick**, you are not well.
बीमार/तंग आया हुआ

*He's very **sick** and needs a doctor.*

side *noun*
sides

1   The **side** of something is a place to the left or right of it.
पहलू

*On the left **side** of the door there's a door bell.*

2   The **side** of something is also its edge.
किनारा

*A square has four **sides**.*

3   The different **sides** in a game are the groups of people who are playing against each other.
पक्ष

*Both **sides** want to win the match.*

a
b
c
d
e
f
g
h
i
j
k
l
m
n
o
p
q
r
s
t
u
v
w
x
y
z

sign *noun*
signs

1 A **sign** is a mark or a shape that has a special meaning.
चिह्न
*In maths, + is a plus **sign** and - is a minus **sign**.*

2 You can also make a **sign** to somebody by moving something.
संकेत
*They gave me a **sign** to show that everything was all right.*

silent *adjective*

1 If you are **silent**, you are not talking.
चुप/ख़ामोश
*She was **silent** because she did not know what to say.*

2 If something is **silent**, it is quiet, with no sound at all.
शांत/ निःशब्द
*The room was **silent**.*

silly *adjective*
sillier, silliest

If you are **silly**, you do not behave in a sensible way.
बेवक़ूफ़ाना
*Don't be **silly**!*

silver *noun*

Silver is a valuable metal.
चाँदी
*He bought her a bracelet made from **silver**.*

sing *verb*
sings, singing, sang, sung

When you **sing**, you make music with your voice.
गाना
*I love **singing**.*

sink *noun*
sinks

A **sink** is a large fixed container in a kitchen or a bathroom that you can fill with water.
सिंक
*The **sink** was filled with dirty dishes.*

sister *noun*
sisters

Your **sister** is a girl or woman who has the same parents as you.
बहन
*This is my **sister**.*

sit *verb*
sits, sitting, sat

If you are **sitting** in a chair, your bottom is resting on the chair and the top part of your body is straight.
बैठना
*Mum was **sitting** in her chair in the kitchen.*

six

Six is the number .
छह

size *noun*
sizes

The **size** of something is how big or small it is.
आकार/माप
*The **size** of the room is about five metres by seven metres.*

skate *noun*
skates

Skates are boots with a thin metal bar on the bottom for moving quickly on ice.
स्केट

skeleton *noun*
skeletons

A **skeleton** is all the bones in a person's or animal's body.
कंकाल
*A human **skeleton** has more than 200 bones.*

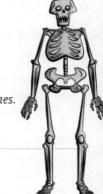

skies

⇨ Look at **sky**.
*The **skies** were grey.*

skill noun

If you have **skill** you are able to do something well.
कौशल
*He shows great **skill** on the football field.*

skin noun
skins

1 Your **skin** covers your whole body.
त्वचा
*Too much sun can damage your **skin**.*

2 The **skin** of a fruit or vegetable covers the outside of it.
छिलका
*She slipped on a banana **skin**.*

skip verb
skips, skipping, skipped

1 If you **skip** along, you move along jumping from one foot to the other.
कूदना
*We **skipped** down the street.*

2 If you **skip** something, you decide not to do it.
छोड़ना
*Don't **skip** breakfast.*

skirt noun
skirts

A **skirt** is something that women and girls wear. It hangs down from the waist and covers part of the legs.
घाघरा

skull noun
skulls

A person's or animal's **skull** is the bones of their head.
खोपड़ी
*Your **skull** protects your brain.*

sky noun
skies

The **sky** is the space around the Earth which you can see when you look up.
आसमान
*The sun was shining in the **sky**.*

sleep verb
sleeps, sleeping, slept

If you **sleep**, you rest with your eyes closed and you do not move.
नींद
*Be quiet! The baby is **sleeping**.*

sleeve noun
sleeves

The **sleeves** of something you wear are the parts that cover your arms.
बाँह
*She wore a blue dress with long **sleeves**.*

slept

⇨ Look at **sleep**.
*She **slept** for three hours.*

slice noun
slices

A **slice** of something is a thin piece that you cut from a larger piece.
फाँक/टुकड़ा
*Would you like a **slice** of bread?*

slide verb
slides, sliding, slid

When someone or something **slides**, they move quickly over a surface.
फिसलना/सरकना
*She **slid** across the ice on her stomach.*

slip verb
slips, slipping, slipped

If you **slip**, you slide and fall.
फिसलना/रपटना
*He **slipped** on the wet grass.*

slipper noun
slippers

Slippers are loose, soft shoes that you wear indoors.
हवाई चप्पल
*She put on a pair of **slippers**.*

a
b
c
d
e
f
g
h
i
j
k
l
m
n
o
p
q
r
s
t
u
v
w
x
y
z

slippery *adjective*

If something is **slippery**, it is smooth or wet, and is difficult to walk on or to hold.
फिसलन भरा/रपटीला
*Be careful—the floor is **slippery**.*

slope *noun*
slopes

A **slope** is the side of a mountain, hill, or valley.
ढाल
*A steep **slope** leads to the beach.*

slow *adjective*
slower, slowest

If something is **slow**, it does not move quickly.
धीमा
*The bus was very **slow**.*

slowly

If something moves **slowly**, it does not move quickly.
धीरे-से

slug *noun*
slugs

A **slug** is a small animal with a long soft body and no legs that moves very slowly.
बिना आवरण का घोंघा

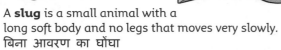

small *adjective*
smaller, smallest

If something is **small**, it is not large in size or amount.
छोटा
*She is **small** for her age.*

smash *verb*
smashes, smashing, smashed

If you **smash** something, it breaks into many pieces.
टकराना/टुकड़े-टुकड़े करना
*The plate **smashed** when it hit the floor.*

smell *noun*
smells

The **smell** of something is what you notice about it when you breathe in through your nose.
गंध
*There was a horrible **smell** in the fridge.*

smile *verb*
smiles, smiling, smiled

If you **smile**, the corners of your mouth turn up because you are happy or you think that something is funny.
मुस्कुराहट
*He **smiled** at me.*

smoke *noun*

Smoke is the black or white clouds of gas that you see in the air when something burns.
धुआँ
*Thick black **smoke** blew over the city.*

smooth *adjective*
smoother, smoothest

Something **smooth** has no rough parts, lumps, or holes.
चिकना
*The baby's skin was soft and **smooth**.*

snail *noun*
snails

A **snail** is a small animal with a long, soft body, no legs, and a round shell on its back.
घोंघा

snake *noun*
snakes

A **snake** is a long, thin animal with no legs, that slides along the ground.
साँप

sneeze *verb*
sneezes, sneezing, sneezed

When you **sneeze**, you suddenly take in air and then blow it down your nose in a noisy way.
छींक मारना
*Cover your nose and mouth when you **sneeze**.*

snow *noun*

Snow is pieces of soft white frozen water that fall from the sky.
बर्फ़

*Six inches of **snow** fell last night.*

soap *noun*

Soap is something that you use with water for washing yourself.
साबुन

*She bought a bar of **soap**.*

sock *noun*
socks

Socks are pieces of cloth that you wear over your foot and ankle, inside your shoes.
मोज़ा

*I have a pair of red **socks**.*

sofa *noun*
sofas

A **sofa** is a long, comfortable seat with a back, that two or three people can sit on.
सोफ़ा

soft *adjective*
softer, softest

1 Something that is **soft** is nice to touch, and not rough or hard.
मुलायम
*She wiped the baby's face with a **soft** cloth.*

2 A **soft** sound or light is very gentle.
हलका/मृदु
*There was a **soft** tapping on my door.*

soil *noun*

Soil is the top layer on the surface of the earth in which plants grow.
मिट्टी

*The **soil** here is good for growing vegetables.*

sold

⇨ Look at **sell**.
*They **sold** their house today.*

soldier *noun*
soldiers

A **soldier** is someone who is in an army.
योद्धा

solid *adjective*

1 Something that is **solid** stays the same shape if it is in a container or not.
ठोस

2 Something that is **solid** is not hollow.
ठोस
*They had to cut through 5 feet of **solid** rock.*

some

You use **some** to talk about an amount of something.
कुछ
*Can I have **some** orange juice please?*

somebody

You use **somebody** to talk about a person without saying who you mean.
कोई

someone

You use **someone** to talk about a person without saying who you mean.
कोई
*I need **someone** to help me.*

something

You use **something** to talk about a thing without saying what it is.
कुछ/कोई चीज़
*He knew that there was **something** wrong.*

sometimes

You use **sometimes** to talk about things that do not take place all the time.
कभी-कभी
***Sometimes** he's a little rude.*

a
b
c
d
e
f
g
h
i
j
k
l
m
n
o
p
q
r
s
t
u
v
w
x
y
z

A
B
C
D
E
F
G
H
I
J
K
L
M
N
O
P
Q
R
S
T
U
V
W
X
Y
Z

somewhere

You use **somewhere** to talk about a place without saying where you mean.

कहीं

*I've seen him before **somewhere**.*

son *noun*
sons

Someone's **son** is their male child.

बेटा

*His **son** is seven years old.*

song *noun*
songs

A **song** is words and music sung together.

गाना

*She sang a **song**.*

soon *adjective*
sooner, soonest

If you are going to do something **soon** you will do it a very short time from now.

जल्दी ही

*I'll call you **soon**.*

sore *adjective*
sorer, sorest

If part of your body is **sore**, it is painful.

पीड़ादायक

*I had a **sore** throat.*

sorry *adjective*
sorrier, sorriest

1 If you are **sorry** about something, you feel sad about it.
   खिन्न/खेदपूर्ण
   *I'm **sorry** he's gone.*

2 If you feel **sorry** for someone, you feel sad for them.
   दु:खी/खेदपूर्ण
   *I felt **sorry** for him because nobody listened to him.*

sort *noun*
sorts

The different **sorts** of something are the different types of it.

प्रकार

*What **sort** of school do you go to?*

sound *noun*
sounds

A **sound** is something that you hear.

ध्वनि

*He heard the **sound** of a car engine outside.*

soup *noun*

Soup is liquid food made by boiling meat, fish, or vegetables in water.

झोल

sour *adjective*

Something that is **sour** has a sharp, nasty taste.

खट्टा

*Lemons have a **sour** taste.*

south *noun*

The **south** is the direction to your right when you are looking towards the place where the sun rises.

दक्षिण

space *noun*
spaces

1 You use **space** to talk about an area that is empty.
   जगह
   *They cut down trees to make **space** for houses.*

2 **Space** is the area past the Earth, where the stars and planets are.
   अंतरिक्ष
   *The six astronauts will spend ten days in **space**.*

spade *noun*
spades

A **spade** is a tool that is used for digging.

कुदाल

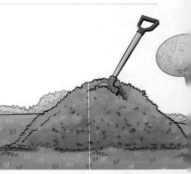

speak *verb*
speaks, speaking, spoken

When you **speak**, you say words.

बोलना

*He **spoke** in a whisper.*

special *adjective*

Someone or something that is **special** is better or more important than other people or things.
ख़ास/विशेष
*Mum made a **special** cake for my birthday.*

speed *noun*
speeds

The **speed** of something is how fast it moves or is done.
गति
*He drove off at high **speed**.*

spell *verb*
spells, spelling, spelled or spelt

When you **spell** a word, you write or say each letter in the correct order.
अक्षर दर अक्षर बोलना या लिखना
*He **spelled** his name.*

spend *verb*
spends, spending, spent

1 When you **spend** money, you buy things with it.
   खर्च करना
   *I have **spent** all my money.*

2 To **spend** time or energy is to use it doing something.
   व्यय करना/बिताना
   *She **spends** hours working on her garden.*

spider *noun*
spiders

A **spider** is a small animal with eight legs.
मकड़ी

spill *verb*
spills, spilling, spilled or spilt

If you **spill** a liquid, you make it flow over the edge of a container by accident.
छलकना/छलकाना
*He always **spilled** the drinks.*

spin *verb*
spins, spinning, spun

If something **spins**, it turns around quickly.
घूमना
*He made the coin **spin** on his desk.*

spine *noun*
spines

Your **spine** is the row of bones down your back.
मेरुदंड

splash *verb*
splashes, splashing, splashed

If you **splash** in water, you hit the water in a noisy way.
छपछपाना
*The children **splashed** around in the water.*

spoil *verb*
spoils, spoiling, spoiled or spoilt

1 If you **spoil** something, you damage it or stop it from working as it should.
   बिगाड़ देना
   *Don't **spoil** the surprise.*

2 If you **spoil** children, you give them everything they want or ask for.
   लाड़-प्यार से बिगाड़ना
   *She acted like a **spoilt** child.*

a
b
c
d
e
f
g
h
i
j
k
l
m
n
o
p
q
r
s
t
u
v
w
x
y
z

127

spoke *noun*
spokes

The **spokes** of a wheel are the bars which join the outside ring to the centre.
तीली/छड़

spoke

⇨ Look at **speak**.
*She **spoke** in a loud voice.*

spoken

⇨ Look at **speak**.
*He has **spoken** to us.*

spoon *noun*
spoons

A **spoon** is a long tool with a round end that is used for eating, serving or mixing food.
चम्मच
*He stirred his coffee with a **spoon**.*

sport *noun*
sports

Sports are games which need energy and skill.
खेल-कूद
*She is very good at **sport**.*

spot *noun*
spots

Spots are small, round areas on a surface.
धब्बा
*The leaves are yellow with orange **spots**.*

spot *verb*
spots, spotting, spotted

If you **spot** something or someone, you notice them.
देखना/खोजना
*I didn't **spot** the mistake in his work.*

spout *noun*
spouts

A **spout** is a tube for pouring liquid.
टोंटी
*My kettle has a long **spout**.*

spray *noun*
sprays

Spray is a lot of small drops of water that are thrown into the air.
फुहार
*The **spray** from the waves covered them.*

spread *verb*
spreads, spreading, spread

1 If you **spread** something somewhere, you open it out.
फैलाना
*She **spread** a towel on the sand and lay on it.*

2 If you **spread** something on a surface, you put it all over the surface.
फैलाना
*She was **spreading** butter on the bread.*

3 If something **spreads**, it reaches a larger area.
फैलना
*The news **spread** quickly.*

spring *noun*
springs

1 **Spring** is the season between winter and summer when the weather becomes warmer and plants start to grow again.
बसंत
*They are getting married next **spring**.*

2 A **spring** is a long piece of metal that goes round and round. It goes back to the same shape after you pull it.
स्प्रिंग
*The **springs** in the bed were old.*

spun

⇨ Look at **spin**.
*He **spun** the wheel.*

square *noun*
squares

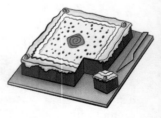

A **square** is a shape with four straight sides that are all the same length.
वर्ग
*Cut the cake in **squares**.*

squirrel *noun*
squirrels

A **squirrel** is a small animal with a long thick tail. **Squirrels** live in trees.
गिलहरी

stable *noun*
stables

A **stable** is a building where people keep horses.
अस्तबल

stairs *noun*

Stairs are steps you walk down or up in a building.
सीढ़ियाँ

*He walked up the **stairs**.*

stamp *noun*
stamps

A **stamp** is a small piece of paper that you stick on an envelope before you post it.
टिकट

*She put a **stamp** on the corner of the envelope.*

stamp *verb*
stamps, stamping, stamped

If you **stamp** your foot, you put your foot down very hard on the ground.
पैर पटकना

*I **stamped** my feet to keep warm.*

stand *verb*
stands, standing, stood

When you are **standing**, you are on your feet.
खड़े रहना

*She was **standing** beside my bed.*

star *noun*
stars

1 A **star** is a large ball of burning gas in space. **Stars** look like small points of light in the sky.
तारा

***Stars** lit the sky.*

2 A **star** is a shape that has four, five, or more points sticking out of it in a pattern.
तारे की आकृति

*How many **stars** are there on the flag?*

3 A **star** is somebody who is famous for doing something, for example acting or singing.
ख्यातिप्राप्त व्यक्ति

*He's one of the **stars** of a TV show.*

start *verb*
starts, starting, started

1 When something **starts**, it begins.
आरंभ होना
*When does the film **start**?*

2 If you **start** to do something, you begin to do it.
आरंभ करना
*She **started** to read her book.*

station *noun*
stations

A **station** is a place where trains or buses stop so that people can get on or off.
स्टेशन/अड्डा

*We went to the train **station**.*

stay *verb*
stays, staying, stayed

1 If you **stay** in a place, you do not move away from it.
बना रहना
*She **stayed** in bed until noon.*

2 If you **stay** somewhere, you live there for a short time.
ठहरना
*He **stayed** with them for two weeks.*

steady *adjective*
steadier, steadiest

Something that is **steady** is firm and not shaking.
सधा हुआ/स्थिर
*He held out a **steady** hand.*

steal *verb*
steals, stealing, stole, stolen

If you **steal** something from someone, you take it without asking or telling them and don't give it back.
चुराना
*They said he **stole** a bicycle.*

a
b
c
d
e
f
g
h
i
j
k
l
m
n
o
p
q
r
s
t
u
v
w
x
y
z

A
B
C
D
E
F
G
H
I
J
K
L
M
N
O
P
Q
R
S
T
U
V
W
X
Y
Z

steam *noun*

Steam is the hot gas that water becomes when it boils.
भाप
*The **steam** rose into the air.*

steel *noun*

Steel is a very strong metal that is made from iron.
इस्पात
*The door is made of **steel**.*

steep *adjective*
steeper, steepest

A **steep** slope rises quickly and is difficult to go up.
खड़ा
*Some of the hills are very **steep**.*

stem *noun*
stems

The **stem** of a plant is the long, thin part that the flowers and leaves grow on.
तना/डंठल
*He cut the **stem** and gave her the flower.*

step *noun*
steps

1 If you take a **step**, you lift your foot and put it down in a different place.
कदम
*I took a **step** towards him.*

2 A **step** is a flat surface that you put your feet on to walk up or down to somewhere.
सीढ़ी
*We went down the **steps** into the garden.*

stick *noun*
sticks

A **stick** is a long, thin piece of wood.
छड़ी
*She put some dry **sticks** on the fire.*

stick *verb*
sticks, sticking, stuck

If you **stick** one thing to another, you join them together using glue.
चिपकाना
*Now **stick** your picture on a piece of paper.*

stiff *adjective*
stiffer, stiffest

Something that is **stiff** is firm and is not easy to bend.
कड़ा
*The sheet of cardboard was **stiff**.*

still *adjective*
stiller, stillest

If you are **still**, you are not moving.
अचल/स्थिर
*Please stand **still**.*

sting *verb*
stings, stinging, stung

If a plant, an animal, or an insect **stings** you, a part of it is pushed into your skin so that you feel a sharp pain.
डंक मारना
*She was **stung** by a bee.*

stir *verb*
stirs, stirring, stirred

When you **stir** a liquid, you move it around using a spoon or a stick.
मिलाना

stole

⇨ Look at **steal**.
*They **stole** our car last night.*

stolen

⇨ Look at **steal**.
*All of her money was **stolen**.*

stomach *noun*
stomachs

Your **stomach** is the place inside your body where food goes when you eat it.
आमाशय
*His **stomach** felt full after the meal.*

stone *noun*
stones

1 **Stone** is a hard solid material that is found in the ground. It is often used for building.
पत्थर
*The floor was solid **stone**.*

2 A **stone** is a small piece of rock that is found on the ground.
पत्थर/कंकड़
*He took a **stone** out of his shoe.*

stood

⇨ Look at **stand**.
*He **stood** in the street.*

stop *verb*
stops, stopping, stopped

1 If you **stop** doing something, you do not do it any more.
रोकना
***Stop** throwing those stones!*

2 If something **stops**, it does not do what it did any more.
रुक जाना
*The rain has **stopped**.*

store *verb*
stores, storing, stored

If you **store** something, you keep it somewhere safe.
संग्रह करना

storm *noun*
storms

A **storm** is very bad weather, with heavy rain and strong winds.
तूफ़ान
*There will be **storms** along the East Coast.*

story *noun*
stories

When someone tells you a **story** they describe people and things that are not real, in a way that makes you enjoy hearing about them.
कहानी
*I'm going to tell you a **story** about four little rabbits.*

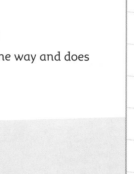

straight *adjective*
straighter, straightest

If something is **straight**, it goes one way and does not bend.
सीधा
*The boat moved in a **straight** line.*

strange *adjective*
stranger, strangest

Something that is **strange** is unusual.
विचित्र
*I had a **strange** dream last night.*

straw *noun*
straws

1 **Straw** is the dry, yellow stems of crops.
भूसा
*The floor of the barn was covered with **straw**.*

2 A **straw** is a thin tube that you use to suck a drink into your mouth.
पेय पीने की नली
*I drank my milk through a **straw**.*

strawberry *noun*
strawberries

A **strawberry** is a small soft red fruit that has a lot of very small seeds on its skin.
स्ट्रॉबेरी

stream *noun*
streams

A **stream** is a small narrow river.
धारा/छोटी नदी
*There was a **stream** at the end of the garden.*

a
b
c
d
e
f
g
h
i
j
k
l
m
n
o
p
q
r
s
t
u
v
w
x
y
z

A
B
C
D
E
F
G
H
I
J
K
L
M
N
O
P
Q
R
S
T
U
V
W
X
Y
Z

street *noun*
streets

A **street** is a road in a city or a town.
गली

*The **streets** were full of people.*

strength *noun*

Your **strength** is how strong you are.
ताक़त

*Swimming builds up the **strength** of your muscles.*

stretch *verb*
stretches, stretching, stretched

1 Something that **stretches** over an area covers all of it.
फैलना

*The line of cars **stretched** for miles.*

2 When you **stretch**, you hold out part of your body as far as you can.
अंगड़ाई लेना

*He yawned and **stretched**.*

strict *adjective*
stricter, strictest

A **strict** person expects people to obey rules.
सख़्त

*My parents are very **strict**.*

string *noun*
strings

1 **String** is thin rope that is made of twisted threads.
रस्सी

*He held out a small bag tied with **string**.*

2 The **strings** on an instrument are the thin pieces of wire that are stretched across it and that make sounds when the instrument is played.
तार

*He changed a guitar **string**.*

strip *noun*
strips

A **strip** of something is a long, narrow piece of it.
पट्टी

*Cut a **strip** off a piece of paper, then twist it and stick the two ends together. Then cut it along the middle and see what happens.*

stripe *noun*
stripes

A **stripe** is a long line that is a different colour from the areas next to it.
धारी

*She wore a blue skirt with white **stripes**.*

strong *adjective*
stronger, strongest

1 Someone who is **strong** is healthy with good muscles.
शक्तिशाली

*I'm not **strong** enough to carry him.*

2 **Strong** things are not easy to break.
मज़बूत

*This **strong** plastic will not crack.*

stuck *adjective*

1 If something is **stuck** in a place, it cannot move.
अटका हुआ

*His car got **stuck** in the snow.*

2 If you get **stuck**, you can't go on doing something because it is too difficult.
अटका हुआ

*The teacher will help if you get **stuck**.*

stung

⇨ Look at **sting**.

*He was **stung** by a wasp.*

submarine *noun*
submarines

A **submarine** is a ship that can travel under the sea.
पनडुब्बी

subtraction *noun*

Subtraction is when you take one number away from another.
घटाव

suck *verb*
sucks, sucking, sucked

If you **suck** something, you hold it in your mouth for a long time.
चूसना
*They **sucked** their sweets.*

sudden *adjective*

Something **sudden** is quick and is not expected.
अचानक
*The car came to a **sudden** stop.*

suddenly

Suddenly is quickly, without being expected.
अचानक से/एकाएक
Suddenly there was a loud bang.

sugar *noun*

Sugar is a sweet thing that is used for making food and drinks taste sweet.
चीनी
*Do you take **sugar** in your coffee?*

suit *noun*
suits

A **suit** is a jacket and trousers or a skirt that are made from the same cloth.
सूट
*He was wearing a dark **suit**.*

sum *noun*
sums

1 A **sum** of money is an amount of money.
राशि
*Large **sums** of money were lost.*

2 In maths, a **sum** is a problem you work out using numbers.
गणित के सवाल
*I have to finish these **sums**.*

summer *noun*
summers

Summer is the season after spring and before autumn. In the **summer** the weather is usually warm or hot.
ग्रीष्म ऋतु

sun *noun*
suns

The **sun** is the large ball of burning gas in the sky that gives us light.
सूर्य
*The **sun** was now high in the sky.*

Sunday *noun*
Sundays

Sunday is the day after Saturday and before Monday.
रविवार
*We went for a drive on **Sunday**.*

sunflower *noun*
sunflowers

A **sunflower** is a very tall plant with large yellow flowers.
सूरजमुखी

sung

⇨ Look at **sing**.
*She has **sung** the song many times before.*

sunk

⇨ Look at **sink**.
*The rock has **sunk** to the bottom of the river.*

sunny *adjective*
sunnier, sunniest

When it is **sunny**, the sun is shining.
धूप से भरा
*The weather was warm and **sunny**.*

a b c d e f g h i j k l m n o p q r s t u v w x y z

A
B
C
D
E
F
G
H
I
J
K
L
M
N
O
P
Q
R
S
T
U
V
W
X
Y
Z

sunshine *noun*

Sunshine is the light that comes from the sun.
धूप
*She was sitting outside in bright **sunshine**.*

supermarket *noun*
supermarkets

A **supermarket** is a large shop that sells all kinds of food and other things for the home.
सुपर बाज़ार
*Lots of people buy food in a **supermarket**.*

sure *adjective*

If you are **sure** that something is true, you know that it is true.
सुनिश्चित
*I am **sure** my answer is correct.*

surface *noun*
surfaces

The **surface** of something is the flat top part of it or the outside of it.
सतह
*There were pen marks on the table's **surface**.*

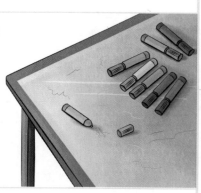

surname *noun*
surnames

Your **surname** is your last name which you share with other people in your family.
कुलनाम

surprise *noun*
surprises

A **surprise** is something that you do not expect.
आश्चर्य
*I have a **surprise** for you!*

swallow *verb*
swallows, swallowing, swallowed

If you **swallow** something, you make it go from your mouth down into your stomach.
निगलना
*She took a bite of the apple and **swallowed** it.*

swam

⇨ Look at **swim**.
*She **swam** across the river.*

swan *noun*
swans

A **swan** is a large bird with a long neck, that lives on rivers and lakes.
हंस

sweep *verb*
sweeps, sweeping, swept

If you **sweep** an area, you push dirt off it using a brush with a long handle.
झाड़ू लगाना
*The man in the shop was **sweeping** the floor.*

sweet *adjective*
sweeter, sweetest

Sweet food and drink has a lot of sugar in it.
मीठा
*Mum gave me a cup of **sweet** tea.*

sweet *noun*
sweets

Sweets are foods that have a lot of sugar.
मिठाई
*Don't eat too many **sweets**.*

swept

⇨ Look at **sweep**.

*The rubbish was **swept** away.*

swim *verb*

swims, swimming, swam, swum

When you **swim**, you move through water by moving your arms and legs.
तैरना

*She learned to **swim** when she was three.*

swing *verb*

swings, swinging, swung

If something **swings**, it keeps moving backwards and forwards or from side to side through the air.
झूलना/डोलना

*She walked beside him with her arms **swinging**.*

switch *noun*

switches

A **switch** is a small button for turning something on or off.
बिजली का बटन

*She pressed the **switch** to turn on the light.*

sword *noun*

swords

A **sword** is like a long knife, with a handle and a long sharp blade.
तलवार

swum

⇨ Look at **swim**.

*He had never **swum** so far.*

swung

⇨ Look at **swing**.

*She **swung** her bag backwards and forwards.*

table *noun*

tables

A **table** is a piece of furniture that has legs and a flat top.
मेज़

tadpole *noun*

tadpoles

A **tadpole** is a small black animal with a round head and a long tail that lives in water. **Tadpoles** grow into frogs or toads.
मेंढक का डिंभ

tail *noun*

tails

An animal's **tail** is the long, thin part at the end of its body.
पूँछ

take *verb*

takes, taking, took, taken

1 If you **take** something, you move it or carry it.
   लेना
   *She **took** the plates into the kitchen.*

2 If you **take** something that does not belong to you, you steal it.
   ले लेना/ चुरा लेना
   *Someone **took** all our money.*

3 If you **take** a vehicle, you ride in it from one place to another.
   लेना/पकड़ना
   *We **took** the bus to school.*

talk *verb*

talks, talking, talked

When you **talk**, you say things to someone.
बात करना

*She **talked** to him on the phone.*

tall *adjective*
taller, tallest

If a person or thing is **tall**, they are higher than usual from top to bottom.
लंबा

*It was a very **tall** building.*

tame *adjective*
tamer, tamest

If an animal or bird is **tame**, it is not afraid of people and will not try to hurt them.
पालतू

tap *verb*
taps, tapping, tapped

If you **tap** something, you hit it but you do not use a lot of strength.
थपथपाना

*He **tapped** on the door and went in.*

tape *noun*

Tape is a long, thin strip of plastic that has glue on one side. You use **tape** to stick things together.
टेप/चिपकाने की पट्टी

*He wrapped the parcel with paper and **tape**.*

taste *verb*
tastes, tasting, tasted

If you **taste** something, you eat or drink a small amount of it to see what it is like.
चखना

*She **tasted** the soup and then added some salt.*

taught

⇨ Look at **teach**.
*My mum **taught** me to read.*

tea *noun*

1 **Tea** is a drink. You make it by pouring hot water on to the dry leaves of a plant called the **tea** bush.
चाय

2 **Tea** is also a meal that you eat in the afternoon or the early evening.
नाश्ता

teach *verb*
teaches, teaching, taught

If you **teach** someone something, you help them to understand it or you show them how to do it.
सिखाना

*He **teaches** people how to play the piano.*

teacher *noun*
teachers

A **teacher** is a person whose job is to teach other people. **Teachers** usually work in schools.
शिक्षक

team *noun*
teams

A **team** is a group of people who work together, or who play a sport together against another group.
टोली

*He is in the school football **team**.*

tear *noun*
tears

Tears are the liquid that comes out of your eyes when you cry.
आँसू

*Her face was wet with **tears**.*

tear *verb*
tears, tearing, tore, torn

If you **tear** something, you pull it into pieces or make a hole in it.
फाड़ना

*Try not to **tear** the paper.*

teeth

⇨ Look at **tooth**.
*Clean your **teeth** before you go to bed.*

telephone *noun*
telephones

A **telephone** is a machine that you use to talk to someone who is in another place.
दूरभाष

television *noun*
televisions

A **television** is a machine that shows moving pictures with sound on a screen.
टेलीविज़न

tell *verb*
tells, telling, told

1 If you **tell** someone something, you let them know about it.
बतलाना
Tell me about your holiday.

2 If you **tell** someone to do something, you say that they must do it.
कहना/आज्ञा देना
*She **told** me to go away.*

3 If you can **tell** something, you know it.
कहना/बतलाना
*I can **tell** that he is angry.*

ten *noun*

Ten is the number **10**.
दस

tent *noun*
tents

A **tent** is made of strong material that is held up with long pieces of metal and ropes. You sleep in a **tent** when you stay in a camp.
तंबू

term *noun*
terms

A **term** is one of the parts of a school year. There are usually three **terms** in a year.
सत्र

terrible *adjective*

If something is **terrible**, it is very bad.
बहुत खराब/भयानक
*That was a **terrible** film.*

test *verb*
tests, testing, tested

If you **test** something, you try it to see what it is like, or how it works.
परखना/जाँचना
Test the water to see if it is warm.

test *noun*
tests

A **test** is something you do to show how much you know or what you can do.
परीक्षा/परख
*The teacher gave us a maths **test**.*

thank *verb*
thanks, thanking, thanked

When you **thank** someone, you tell them that you are pleased about something they have given you or have done for you. You usually do this by saying "Thank you".
धन्यवाद देना
*I **thanked** him for my present.*

theatre *noun*
theatres

A **theatre** is a building where you go to see people acting stories, singing, or dancing.
नाट्यगृह

their

You use **their** to say that something belongs to a group of people, animals, or things.
उनका
*They took off **their** coats.*

theirs

You use **theirs** to say that something belongs to a group of people, animals, or things.
उनका
*The house next to **theirs** was empty.*

then

1 **Then** means at that time.
तब
*He wasn't as rich **then** as he is now.*

2 You also use **then** to say that one thing happens after another.
फिर/बाद में
*She said good night, **then** went to bed.*

there

1 You use **there** to say that something is in a place or is happening, or to make someone notice it.
उधर
There are flowers on the table.

2 **There** also means to a place, or at a place.
वहाँ
*I have never been **there** before.*

there's

There's is short for **there is**.
वहाँ है'
There's nothing in the box.

they

You use **they** when you are talking about more than one person, animal, or thing.
वे
They are all in the same class.

they'd

1 **They'd** is short for **they had**.
उन्होंने किया है

2 **They'd** is also short for **they would**.
वे करेंगे
*The boys said **they'd** come back later.*

they'll

They'll is short for **they will**.
वे करेंगे
They'll be here on Monday.

they're

They're is short for **they are**.
वे हैं
They're going to the circus.

they've

They've is short for **they have**.
वे कर चुके हैं
They've gone away.

thick *adjective*
thicker, thickest

1 If something is **thick**, it is deep or wide between one side and the other.
मोटा
*He cut a **thick** slice of bread.*

2 If a liquid is **thick**, it flows slowly.
गाढ़ा
*This soup is very **thick**.*

thigh *noun*
thighs

Your **thighs** are the parts of your legs that are above your knees.
जांघ
*His **thighs** ached from climbing the hill.*

thin *adjective*
thinner, thinnest

1 If something is **thin**, it is narrow between one side and the other.
पतला
*The book is printed on very **thin** paper.*

2 If a person or animal is **thin**, they are not fat and they do not weigh much.
दुबला
*He was a tall, **thin** man.*

thing *noun*
things

A **thing** is something that is not a plant, an animal, or a human being.
चीज़
*What's that **thing** lying in the road?*

think *verb*
thinks, thinking, thought

1 If you **think** something, you believe that it is true.
मानना
*I **think** it's a great idea.*

2 When you **think**, you use your mind.
सोचना
*I tried to **think** what to do.*

thirsty *adjective*
thirstier, thirstiest

If you are **thirsty**, you want to drink something.
प्यासा

thought

⟹ Look at **think**.
*I **thought** they were here.*

thread *noun*
threads

Thread is a long, thin piece of cotton or wool that you use to sew cloth.
धागा

three *noun*

Three is the number .
तीन

threw

⟹ Look at **throw**.
*She **threw** her coat on to a chair.*

throat *noun*
throats

1 Your **throat** is the back part of your mouth that you use to swallow and to breathe.
गला / कंठ

2 Your **throat** is also the front part of your neck.
गला / कंठ

through

Through means going all the way from one side of something to the other side.
के द्वारा
*We walked **through** the forest.*

throw *verb*
throws, throwing, threw, thrown

When you **throw** something you are holding, you move your hand quickly and let the thing go, so that it moves through the air.
फेंकना
***Throw** the ball to me.*

thumb *noun*
thumbs

Your **thumb** is the short, thick finger on the side of your hand.
अँगूठा
*The baby sucked its **thumb**.*

thunder *noun*

Thunder is the loud noise that you sometimes hear from the sky when there is a storm.
गडगड़ाहट

Thursday *noun*
Thursdays

Thursday is the day after Wednesday and before Friday.
वीरवार
*I saw her on **Thursday**.*

a
b
c
d
e
f
g
h
i
j
k
l
m
n
o
p
q
r
s
t
u
v
w
x
y
z

139

A
B
C
D
E
F
G
H
I
J
K
L
M
N
O
P
Q
R
S
T
U
V
W
X
Y
Z

tidy *adjective*
tidier, tidiest

Something that is **tidy** is neat, with everything in its proper place.
साफ़-सुथरा

tie *verb*
ties, tying, tied

If you **tie** something, you fasten it with string or a rope.
बाँधना
*He **tied** the dog to the fence.*

tie *noun*
ties

A **tie** is a long, narrow piece of cloth that you tie a knot in and wear around your neck with a shirt.
टाई

tiger *noun*
tigers

A **tiger** is a large wild cat that has orange fur with black stripes.
चीता

tight *adjective*
tighter, tightest

1 If clothes are **tight**, they are so small that they fit very close to your body.
तंग
*His trousers were very **tight**.*

2 Something that is **tight** is fastened so that it is not easy to move it.
कसा हुआ
*The string was tied in a **tight** knot.*

time *noun*

1 **Time** is how long something takes to happen. We measure **time** in minutes, hours, days, weeks, months, and years.
समय/वक़्त
*I've known him for a long **time**.*

2 The **time** is a moment in the day that you describe in hours and minutes.
समय
*"What **time** is it?"—"Ten past five."*

tin *noun*
tins

1 **Tin** is a kind of soft, pale grey metal.
कलई

2 A **tin** is a metal container for food.
कनस्तर
*She opened a **tin** of beans.*

tiny *adjective*
tinier, tiniest

If something is **tiny**, it is very small.
छोटा
*Our new kitten is **tiny**.*

tired *adjective*

If you are **tired**, you need to rest or get some sleep.
थका हुआ

toad *noun*
toads

A **toad** is a small animal that looks like a frog. **Toads** have rough, dry skin and live on land.
भेक - मेंढक जैसा एक जीव

today

Today means the day that is happening now.
आज
*I feel much better **today**.*

toe *noun*
toes

Your **toes** are the five parts at the end of each foot.
पैर की अंगुलियाँ
*I'm sorry I stood on your **toes**.*

together

If people do something **together**, they do it with each other.
साथ-साथ
*We played football **together**.*

told

⇨ Look at **tell**.
*We **told** them the answer.*

tomato *noun*
tomatoes

A **tomato** is a soft red fruit with a lot of juice.
टमाटर

tomorrow

Tomorrow is the day after today.
आने वाला कल
*I'll see you **tomorrow**.*

tongue *noun*
tongues

Your **tongue** is the soft part inside your mouth that moves when you eat or talk.
जीभ

tonight

Tonight is the evening or night that will come at the end of today.
आज रात को
*We're going out **tonight**.*

too

1 **Too** means also.
भी
*Can I come **too**?*

2 You also use **too** to mean more than you want or need.
बहुत ज़्यादा
*The TV is **too** loud.*

took

⇨ Look at **take**.
*It **took** me hours.*

tool *noun*
tools

A **tool** is something that you hold in your hands and use to do a job.
उपकरण

tooth *noun*
teeth

1 Your **teeth** are the hard, white things in your mouth that you use to bite and chew food.
दाँत
*I clean my **teeth** twice a day.*

2 The **teeth** of a comb, a saw, or a zip are the parts that are in a row along its edge.
दाँता

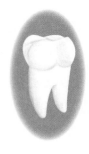

top *noun*
tops

1 The **top** of something is the highest part of it.
शीर्ष भाग
*We climbed to the **top** of the hill.*

2 The **top** of something is also the part that fits over the end of it.
ढक्कन
*He took the **top** off the jar.*

tore

⇨ Look at **tear**.
*She **tore** her dress on a nail.*

torn

⇨ Look at **tear**.
*He has **torn** the cover of the book.*

tortoise *noun*
tortoises

A **tortoise** is an animal with a hard shell on its back. It can pull its head and legs inside the shell. **Tortoises** move very slowly.
कछुआ

touch *verb*
touches, touching, touched

1 If you **touch** something, you put your fingers or your hand on it.
छूना
*The baby **touched** my face.*

2 If one thing **touches** another, they are so close that there is no space between them.
स्पर्श करना
*Her feet **touched** the floor.*

a
b
c
d
e
f
g
h
i
j
k
l
m
n
o
p
q
r
s
t
u
v
w
x
y
z

towards

Towards means in the direction of something.
की तरफ़
*He moved **towards** the door.*

towel *noun*
towels

A **towel** is a piece of thick, soft cloth that you use to get yourself dry.
तौलिया

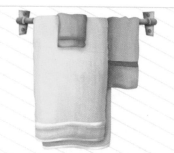

town *noun*
towns

A **town** is a place with a lot of streets, buildings, and shops, where people live and work.
शहर/कस्बा

toy *noun*
toys

A **toy** is something that you play with.
खिलौना

tractor *noun*
tractors

A **tractor** is a vehicle with big wheels at the back. **Tractors** are used on a farm to pull machines and other heavy things.
ट्रैक्टर

traffic *noun*

Traffic is all the vehicles that are on a road at the same time.
यातायात
*There is a lot of **traffic** in the town today.*

train *noun*
trains

A **train** is a long vehicle that is pulled by an engine along a railway line.
रेलगाड़ी

travel *verb*
travels, travelling, travelled

When you **travel**, you go from one place to another.
यात्रा करना
*He **travelled** to many different countries.*

tree *noun*
trees

A **tree** is a very tall plant with branches, leaves, and a hard main part that is called a trunk.
पेड़

triangle *noun*
triangles

1 A **triangle** is a shape with three straight sides.
त्रिकोण

2 A **triangle** is also an instrument made of metal in the shape of a **triangle** that you hit with a stick to make music.
धातु का बना हुआ त्रिभुजाकार वाद्ययंत्र

trick *verb*
tricks, tricking, tricked

If someone **tricks** you, they make you believe something that is not true so that you will do what they want.
बहकाना/चकमा देना
*They **tricked** her into giving them money.*

tried

⇨ Look at **try**.
*They **tried** their best.*

tries

⇨ Look at **try**.
*She **tries** to help.*

trip noun
trips

When you go on a **trip**, you travel to a place and then come back.
भ्रमण/सैर
*We went on a **trip** to the park.*

trousers noun

Trousers are things that you can wear. They cover the part of your body below the waist, and each leg.
पतलून
*He was wearing brown **trousers**.*

truck noun
trucks

A **truck** is a large vehicle that is used to carry things.
ट्रक

true adjective

1 If a story is **true**, it really happened.
सच्चा
*Everything she said was **true**.*

2 If something is **true**, it is right or correct.
सही/सच्चा
*Is it **true** that you have six cats?*

trunk noun
trunks

1 A **trunk** is the thick stem of a tree. The branches and roots grow from the **trunk**.
तना

2 An elephant's **trunk** is its long nose. Elephants use their **trunks** to suck up water and to lift things.
सूँड

3 A **trunk** is also a large, strong box that you use to keep things in.
संदूक

try verb
tries, trying, tried

1 If you **try** to do something, you do it as well as you can.
प्रयास करना
*I will **try** to come tomorrow.*

2 If you **try** something, you test it to see what it is like or how it works.
आज़माना
*Would you like to **try** my new bike?*

tube noun
tubes

1 A **tube** is a long, round, hollow piece of metal, rubber, or plastic.
नली
*The liquid goes through the **tube** into the bottle.*

2 A **tube** is also a soft metal or plastic container that you press to make what is in it come out.
ट्यूब
*He bought a **tube** of glue.*

Tuesday noun
Tuesdays

Tuesday is the day after Monday and before Wednesday.
मंगलवार
*He came home on **Tuesday**.*

tune noun
tunes

A **tune** is a piece of music that is nice to listen to.
धुन
*She played a **tune** on the piano.*

tunnel noun
tunnels

A **tunnel** is a long hole that goes below the ground or through a hill.
सुरंग

a
b
c
d
e
f
g
h
i
j
k
l
m
n
o
p
q
r
s
t
u
v
w
x
y
z

turn *verb*
turns, turning, turned

1   When you **turn**, you move in a different direction.
मुड़ना
*He **turned** and walked away.*

2   When something **turns**, it moves around in a circle.
मुड़ना
*The wheels **turned** slowly.*

3   If one thing **turns** into another thing, it becomes that thing.
बदलना/होना
*The tadpole **turned** into a frog.*

4   When you **turn** a machine on, you make it start working. When you **turn** it off, you make it stop working.
चालू करना/बंद करना
*I **turned** off the television.*

tusk *noun*
tusks

An elephant's **tusks** are the two very long, curved teeth that it has beside its trunk.
गजदंत/हाथी के दाँत

TV *noun*
TVs

TV is short for **television**.
टी वी
*What's on **TV**?*

twelve *noun*

Twelve is the number .
बारह

twice

If something happens **twice**, it happens two times.
दो बार
*I've met him **twice**.*

twig *noun*
twigs

A **twig** is a very small, thin branch that grows on a tree or a bush.
टहनी

twin *noun*
twins

If two people are **twins**, they have the same parents and they were born on the same day. **Twins** often look alike.
जुड़वाँ

twist *verb*
twists, twisting, twisted

If you **twist** something, you turn one end of it in one direction while you hold the other end or turn it in the opposite direction.
मरोड़ना
*She **twisted** the towel in her hands.*

two *noun*

Two is the number .
दो

tying

⇨ Look at **tie**.
*He was **tying** the two pieces of rope together.*

type *noun*
types

A **type** of something is the kind of thing that it is.
प्रकार
*Owls are a **type** of bird.*

type *verb*
types, typing, typed

If you **type** something, you write it with a machine, for example a computer.
टंकित करना
*She **typed** a letter.*

tyre *noun*
tyres

A **tyre** is a thick circle made of strong rubber that goes round a wheel. **Tyres** usually have air inside them.
टायर

A B C D E F G H I J K L M N O P Q R S T U V W X Y Z

ugly *adjective*
uglier, ugliest

If something is **ugly**, it is not nice to look at.

बदसूरत

*The monster had an **ugly** face.*

umbrella *noun*
umbrellas

An **umbrella** is a long stick that is joined to a cover made of cloth or plastic. You hold an **umbrella** over your head so that you will not get wet in the rain.

छाता

uncle *noun*
uncles

Your **uncle** is the brother of your mother or father, or the husband of your aunt.

चाचा/मामा/फूफा/मौसा

understand *verb*
understands, understanding, understood

If you **understand** something, you know what it means or why or how it happens.

समझना

*I didn't **understand** what he said.*

underwear *noun*

Your **underwear** is the name for the clothes that you wear next to your skin, under all your other clothes.

अंतःवस्त्र

undress *verb*
undresses, undressing, undressed

When you **undress**, you take off your clothes.

कपड़े उतारना

uniform *noun*
uniforms

A **uniform** is a special set of clothes that some people wear to show what job they do, or some children wear to show what school they go to.

वर्दी

*I put on my school **uniform**.*

until

If something happens **until** a time, it happens before that time and then stops at that time.

जब तक

*Wait here **until** I come back.*

unusual *adjective*

If something is **unusual**, it does not happen very often.

असामान्य

*It is **unusual** for him to be late.*

up

When something moves **up**, it moves from a lower place to a higher place.

ऊपर

*She ran **up** the stairs.*

upon

Upon means the same as **on**.

के ऊपर

*He stood **upon** the bridge.*

a
b
c
d
e
f
g
h
i
j
k
l
m
n
o
p
q
r
s
t
u
v
w
x
y
z

upset *adjective*

If you are **upset**, you are sad because something bad has happened.
परेशान

*I was **upset** when my brother broke my doll.*

upside down

1 If something is **upside down**, the part that is usually at the bottom is at the top.
उलटा
*The picture was **upside down**.*

2 If you hang **upside down**, your head is below your feet.
उलटा

urgent *adjective*

If something is **urgent**, it is very important and you need to do something about it quickly.
अत्यावश्यक
*This problem is **urgent**.*

use *verb*
uses, using, used

If you **use** something, you do something with it.
इस्तेमाल करना
***Use** a cloth to clean the table.*

useful *adjective*

If something is **useful**, you can use it to do something or to help you in some way.
उपयोगी

usual *adjective*

Something that is **usual** is what happens most often.
आम/सामान्य रूप से
*He arrived at his **usual** time.*

usually

If something **usually** happens, it is the thing that happens most often.
आमतौर पर
*I **usually** take the bus to school.*

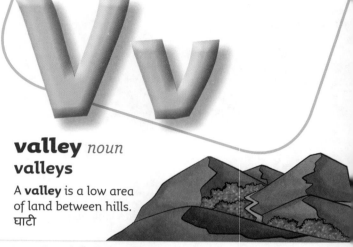

valley *noun*
valleys

A **valley** is a low area of land between hills.
घाटी

valuable *adjective*

If something is **valuable**, it is worth a lot of money.
क़ीमती/मूल्यवान

van *noun*
vans

A **van** is a covered vehicle larger than a car but smaller than a lorry. People use **vans** for carrying things.
वैन

vase *noun*
vases

A **vase** is a jar for flowers.
गुलदान

vegetable *noun*
vegetables

Vegetables are plants that you can cook and eat.
सब्ज़ी

vehicle *noun*
vehicles

A **vehicle** is a machine that carries people or things from one place to another.
वाहन

verb *noun*
verbs

A **verb** is a word like 'sing,' 'feel,' or 'eat' that you use for saying what someone or something does.
क्रिया

very

Very is used before a word to make it stronger.
बहुत
*She had a **very** bad dream.*

vet *noun*
vets

A **vet** is a doctor for animals.
पशु-चिकित्सक

video *noun*
videos

A **video** is a copy of a film or television programme.
वीडियो

village *noun*
villages

A **village** is a small town.
गाँव

voice *noun*
voices

Your **voice** is the sound that comes from your mouth when you talk or sing.
आवाज़

volcano *noun*
volcanoes

A **volcano** is a mountain that throws out hot, liquid rock and fire.
ज्वालामुखी

vote *verb*
votes, voting, voted

When a group of people **vote**, everybody shows what they want to do, usually by writing on a piece of paper or by putting their hands up.
मत देना
*We **voted** to send money to people who were in the earthquake.*

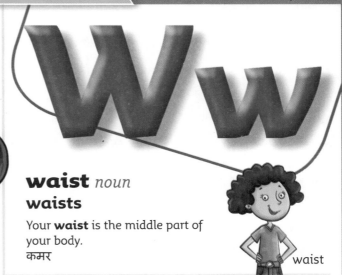

waist *noun*
waists

Your **waist** is the middle part of your body.
कमर

waist

wait *verb*
waits, waiting, waited

When you **wait** for something or someone, you spend time doing very little, before something happens.
प्रतीक्षा करना

wake *verb*
wakes, waking, woke, woken

When you **wake** up, you stop sleeping.
जागना

walk *verb*
walks, walking, walked

When you **walk**, you move along by putting one foot in front of the other.
चलना

wall *noun*
walls

A **wall** is one of the sides of a building or a room.
दीवार

want *verb*
wants, wanting, wanted

If you **want** something, you would like to have it.
चाहना

A
B
C
D
E
F
G
H
I
J
K
L
M
N
O
P
Q
R
S
T
U
V
W
X
Y
Z

war *noun*
wars

A **war** is when countries or groups fight each other.
युद्ध

wardrobe *noun*
wardrobes

A **wardrobe** is a tall cupboard that you can hang your clothes in.
कपड़ों की अलमारी

warm *adjective*
warmer, warmest

Something that is **warm** is not cold, but not hot.
गरम
*The bread is still **warm** from the oven.*

warn *verb*
warns, warning, warned

If you **warn** someone about a possible problem or danger, you tell them about it.
चेतावनी देना
*I **warned** them not to go.*

was

⇨ Look at **be**.
*It **was** my birthday yesterday.*

wash *verb*
washes, washing, washed

If you **wash** something, you clean it using soap and water.
धोना

wasn't

Wasn't is short for **was not**.
नहीं था
*She **wasn't** happy.*

wasp *noun*
wasps

A **wasp** is an insect with wings and yellow and black stripes across its body. **Wasps** can sting people.
ततैया

waste *verb*
wastes, wasting, wasted

If you **waste** time, money, or energy, you use too much of it on something that is not important.
बर्बाद करना/व्यर्थ करना
*It's important not to **waste** water.*

watch *verb*
watches, watching, watched

If you **watch** something, you look at it for a period of time.
देखना

watch *noun*
watches

A **watch** is a small clock that you wear on your wrist.
कलाई घड़ी

water *noun*

Water is a clear liquid that has no colour, taste or smell. It falls from clouds as rain.
पानी

wave *noun*
waves

Waves on the surface of the sea are the parts that move up and down.
लहर
*The **waves** broke over the rocks.*

wave *verb*
waves, waving, waved

If you **wave** your hand, you move it from side to side, usually to say hello or goodbye.
लहराना

wax *noun*

Wax is a soft material that melts when you make it hot. It is used to make crayons and candles.
मोम

way *noun*
ways

1 A **way** of doing something is how you do it.
तरीक़ा
*This is the **way** to throw the ball.*

2 The **way** to a place is how you get there.
रास्ता
*We're going the wrong **way**!*

weak *adjective*
weaker, weakest

If someone or something is **weak**, they are not strong.
कमज़ोर
*When she spoke, her voice was **weak**.*

wear *verb*
wears, wearing, wore, worn

When you **wear** clothes, shoes or glasses, you have them on your body.
पहनना
*What are you going to **wear** today?*

weather *noun*

The **weather** is what it is like outside, for example if it is raining or sunny.
मौसम
*What will the **weather** be like tomorrow?*

web *noun*
webs

1 The **Web** is made up of a very large number of websites all joined together. You can use it anywhere in the world to search for information.
वेब

2 A **web** is the thin net made by a spider from a string that comes out of its body.
मकड़ी का जाला

website *noun*
websites

A **website** is a place on the Internet that gives you information.
वेबसाइट
*Our school has a **website**.*

we'd

1 **We'd** is short for **we had**.
हमने किया है
We'd left early in the morning.

2 **We'd** is also short for **we would**.
हम करेंगे
We'd like you to come with us.

wedding *noun*
weddings

A **wedding** is when two people get married.
विवाह

Wednesday *noun*
Wednesdays

Wednesday is the day after Tuesday and before Thursday.
बुधवार

week *noun*
weeks

A **week** is a period of seven days.
सप्ताह
*This is the last **week** of the holidays.*

weekend *noun*
weekends

The **weekend** is the days at the end of the week, when you do not go to school or work.
सप्ताहांत

weigh *verb*
weighs, weighing, weighed

If you **weigh** something or someone, you measure how heavy they are.
तौलना
*I **weigh** more than my brother.*

a
b
c
d
e
f
g
h
i
j
k
l
m
n
o
p
q
r
s
t
u
v
w
x
y
z

A	
B	
C	

weight *noun*

The **weight** of a person or thing is how heavy they are.
वज़न
*What is your **weight** and height?*

well
better, best

If you do something **well**, you do it in a good way.
बख़ूबी/अच्छी तरह से
*He draws **well**.*

well *noun*

A **well** is a deep hole in the ground from which people take water, oil or gas.
कुआँ

we'll

We'll is short for **we will**.
हम करेंगे
We'll come along later.

we're

We're is short for **we are**.
हम हैं
We're late!

went

➡ Look at **go**.
*They **went** to school.*

were

➡ Look at **be**.
*They **were** at home yesterday.*

weren't

Weren't is short for **were not**.
हम नहीं थे
*They **weren't** at school yesterday.*

west *noun*

The **west** is the direction ahead of you when you are looking towards the place where the sun goes down.
पश्चिम

wet *adjective*
wetter, wettest

If something is **wet**, it is covered in water.
गीला

we've

We've is short for **we have**.
हमने किया है
We've got lots of books.

whale *noun*
whales

Whales are very large sea mammals.
ह्वेल
Whales breathe through a hole on the top of their heads.

what

You use **what** in questions when you ask for information.
क्या
What time is it?

wheat *noun*

Wheat is a crop. People make flour and bread from **wheat**.
गेहूँ

wheel *noun*
wheels

Wheels are round and they turn. Bikes and cars move along on **wheels**.
पहिया

wheelchair *noun*
wheelchairs

A **wheelchair** is a chair with wheels that you use if you cannot walk.
पहियेदार कुर्सी

when

You use **when** to ask what time something happened or will happen.
कब
When are you leaving?

where

You use **where** to ask questions about the place something is in.
कहाँ
Where's your house?

which

You use **which** when you want help to choose between things.
कौन-सा
Which shoes should I put on?

while

If one thing happens **while** another thing is happening, the two things are happening at the same time.
जब तक
She goes to work while her children are at school.

whisper *verb*
whispers, whispering, whispered

When you **whisper**, you speak in a very quiet voice.
फुसफुसाना
Don't you know it's rude to whisper?

whistle *verb*
whistles, whistling, whistled

When you **whistle**, you make sounds like music by blowing hard.
सीटी बजाना

white *noun*

White is the colour of snow or milk.
सफेद
His shirt is white.

who

You use **who** in questions when you ask about someone's name.
कौन
Who won the quiz?

who'd

Who'd is short for **who would**.
कौन करेगा
Who'd like to come with me?

whole *adjective*

The **whole** of something is all of it.
समस्त
Have the whole cake.

who'll

Who'll is short for **who will**.
कौन करेगा
Who'll go and find her?

whose

You use **whose** to ask who something belongs to.
किसका
Whose bag is this?

why

You use **why** when you are asking about the reason for something.
क्यों
Why did you do it?

wide *adjective*
wider, widest

Something that is **wide** is a large distance from one side to the other.
चौड़ा
The bed is too wide for this room.

width *noun*

The **width** of something is the distance from one side to another.
चौड़ाई
Measure the full width of the table.

wife *noun*
wives

A man's **wife** is the woman he is married to.
पत्नी

A
B
C
D
E
F
G
H
I
J
K
L
M
N
O
P
Q
R
S
T
U
V
W
X
Y
Z

wild *adjective*
wilder, wildest

Wild animals or plants live or grow in nature, and people do not take care of them.
वन्य/जंगली

will *verb*

You use **will** to talk about things that are going to happen in the future.
होगा
*Mum **will** be angry.*

win *verb*
wins, winning, won

If you **win**, you do better than everyone.
जीतना
*You've **won** first prize!*

wind *noun*

Wind is air that moves.
हवा

wind *verb*
winds, winding, wound

1 If a road or river **winds**, it twists and turns.
घूम जाना/मुड़ना
2 When you **wind** something long around something, you wrap it around several times.
लपेटना
*She **wound** the rope around her waist.*

window *noun*
windows

A **window** is a space in the wall of a building or in the side of a vehicle that has glass in it.
खिड़की

wing *noun*
wings

The **wings** of birds, insects or aeroplanes are the parts that keep them in the air.
पंख

winner *noun*
winners

The **winner** of a race or competition is the person who wins it.
विजेता
*Our teacher will give the prizes to the **winners**.*

winter *noun*
winters

Winter is the season after autumn and before spring. In the **winter** the weather is usually cold.
शीत ऋतु

wipe *verb*
wipes, wiping, wiped

If you **wipe** dirt or liquid from something, you remove it using a cloth or your hands.
पोंछना
*She **wiped** the tears from her eyes.*

wire *noun*
wires

A **wire** is a long thin piece of metal.
तार
*The birds were sitting on a telephone **wire**.*

wise *adjective*
wiser, wisest

A **wise** person can decide on the right thing to do.
बुद्धिमान

wish *verb*
wishes, wishing, wished

If you **wish** something, you would like it to be true.
इच्छा
*I **wish** I had a pet.*

witch *noun*
witches

In children's stories, a **witch** is a woman who has magic powers that she uses to do bad things.
चुड़ैल/जादूगरनी

with

1 If one person is **with** another, they are together in one place.
साथ

*He's watching a film **with** his friends.*

2 You use **with** to say that someone has something.
से युक्त

*My daughter is the girl **with** brown hair.*

without

If you do something **without** someone, they are not in the same place as you are, or they are not doing the same thing as you.
के बिना

*He went **without** me.*

wives

⇨ Look at **wife**.
*The men bought flowers for their **wives**.*

wizard *noun*
wizards

In children's stories, a **wizard** is a man who has magic powers.
जादूगर

woke

⇨ Look at **wake**.
*They **woke** early.*

woken

⇨ Look at **wake**.
*We were **woken** by a loud noise.*

wolf *noun*
wolves

A **wolf** is a wild animal that looks like a large dog.
भेड़िया

woman *noun*
women

A **woman** is an adult female person.
औरत/महिला

won

⇨ Look at **win**.
*She **won** first prize.*

won't

Won't is short for **will not**.
नहीं होगा

*I **won't** be late.*

wood *noun*
woods

1 **Wood** is the hard material that trees are made of.
लकड़ी

2 A **wood** is a large area of trees growing near each other.
जंगल

wool *noun*

Wool is a material made from the fur of sheep. It is used for making things such as clothes.
ऊन

word *noun*
words

Words are things that you say or write.
शब्द

*Some **words** are short and some are long.*

wore

⇨ Look at **wear**.
*She **wore** a red dress.*

work *verb*
works, working, worked

1 When you **work**, you do something that uses a lot of your time or effort.
काम करना

*We **work** hard all day.*

2 If a machine **works**, it does its job.
काम करना

*The TV isn't **working**.*

a
b
c
d
e
f
g
h
i
j
k
l
m
n
o
p
q
r
s
t
u
v
w
x
y
z

153

A
B
C
D
E
F
G
H
I
J
K
L
M
N
O
P
Q
R
S
T
U
V
W
X
Y
Z

world noun
worlds
The **world** is the earth, the planet we live on.
दुनिया

worm noun
worms
A **worm** is a small animal with a long thin body, no bones, and no legs.
कीड़ा

worn
⇨ Look at **wear**.
*Have you **worn** this?*

worry verb
worries, worrying, worried
If you **worry**, you keep thinking about problems that you have or about nasty things that might happen.
चिंता करना

worse
If something is **worse** than another thing, it is not as good.
बदतर
*My spelling is **worse** than yours.*

worst
If something is the **worst**, all other things are better.
सबसे खराब
*That was the **worst** day in my life.*

worth
If something is **worth** a sum of money, that's how much you could sell it for.
क़ीमत
*This gold ring is **worth** a lot of money.*

would verb
You use **would** to say that someone agreed to do something. You use **would not** to say that they refused to do something.
होगा
*They said they **would** come to my party.*

wound
⇨ Look at **wind**.
*She **wound** the rope around her wrist.*

wrap verb
wraps, wrapping, wrapped
When you **wrap** something, you fold paper or cloth around it to cover it.
लपेटना
*I didn't have enough paper to **wrap** the present.*

wrist noun
wrists
Your **wrist** is the part of your body between your arm and your hand. Your **wrists** bend when you move your hands.
कलाई

write verb
writes, writing, wrote, written
When you **write** something, you use a pen or pencil to make letters, words, or numbers.
लिखना
*He **wrote** his name in the book.*

writing noun
Writing is words that have been written or printed.
लिखावट/लेख
*Can you read my **writing**?*

written
⇨ Look at **write**.
*My uncle has **written** a song.*

wrong adjective
1   If you say that an answer is **wrong**, you mean that it is not right.
    ग़लत
    *No, you've got that **wrong**!*

2   If you say that something someone does is **wrong**, you mean that it is bad.
    बुरा/ख़राब
    *It is **wrong** to hurt animals.*

X-ray *noun*
X-rays

An **X-ray** is a picture of the inside of someone's body.
एक्स-रे
*The **X-ray** showed that my arm was broken.*

xylophone *noun*
xylophones

A **xylophone** is an instrument made of flat pieces of wood or metal in a row. You hit the pieces with a stick to make different sounds.
ज़ाइलोफ़ोन - लकड़ी से बना एक वाद्ययंत्र

yacht *noun*
yachts

A **yacht** is a large boat with sails or an engine, used for races or for making trips.
पाल नौका

yawn *verb*
yawns, yawning, yawned

If you **yawn**, you open your mouth very wide and breathe in more air than usual because you are tired or bored.
जम्हाई लेना

year *noun*
years

A **year** is a period of twelve months, beginning on January 1 and finishing on December 31.
वर्ष

yell *verb*
yells, yelling, yelled

If you **yell**, you shout something, often because you are angry.
चिल्लाना
*She **yelled** at him to stop.*

yellow *noun*

Yellow is the colour of lemons or butter.
पीला
*Her favourite colour is **yellow**.*

yes

You say **yes** to agree with someone or to say that something is true, or if you want something.
हाँ

yesterday

Yesterday is the day before today.
बीता हुआ कल
*There was no school **yesterday**.*

yogurt or yoghurt *noun*
yogurts or yoghurts

Yogurt is a thick liquid food that is made from milk.
दही
*I like strawberry **yogurt** more than peach **yogurt**.*

yolk *noun*
yolks

The **yolk** of an egg is the yellow part.
ज़रदी

you

You means the person or people that someone is talking or writing to.
तुम
*Can I help **you**?*

a b c d e f g h i j k l m n o p q r s t u v w x y z

you'd

1 **You'd** is short for **you had**.
तुमने किया है
*I thought **you'd** told him.*

2 **You'd** is also short for **you would**.
तुम करोगे
***You'd** like it a lot.*

you'll

You'll is short for **you will**.
तुम करोगे
***You'll** be late!*

young *adjective*
younger, youngest

A **young** person, animal, or plant has not lived for very long.
युवा
*A kitten is a **young** cat.*

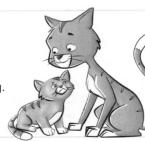

your

You use **your** to show that something belongs to the people that you are talking to.
तुम्हारा
*I do like **your** name.*

you're

You're is short for **you are**.
तुम हो
***You're** very early!*

yours

Yours refers to something belonging to the people that you are talking to.
तुम्हारा
*His hair is longer than **yours**.*

yourself
yourselves

Yourself means you alone.
खुद को
*You'll hurt **yourself**.*

you've

You've is short for **you have**.
***You've** got very long legs.*

zebra *noun*
zebras

A **zebra** is a wild African animal like a horse with black and white stripes.
जेबरा

zero
zeros or zeroes

Zero is the number .
शून्य

zip *noun*
zips

A **zip** is two long rows of little teeth and a piece that slides along them. You pull this to open or close the **zip**.
ज़िप/चेन

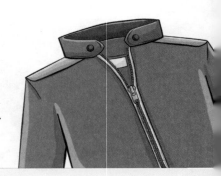

zoo *noun*
zoos

A **zoo** is a place where live animals are kept so that people can look at them.
चिड़ियाघर